Reading a story told aloud is a communal act. Like musical scores that come to life when played, stories take on an added dimension when shared aurally. Carol Birch—storyteller, children's librarian, and teacher—tackles the slippery topic of the difference between reciting a written story from memory, and telling it directly and engagingly to a group of listeners.

We all recognize the difference when we hear it. But how does one bridge it? The same way, Birch asserts, that we take home most prizes: you must be present to win. Meaning, the storyteller must know much, much more about the story than he or she tells. How can you communicate the fortunes of a character you don't know yourself? How can you convey a story whose setting you have not fully imagined?

In addition to her own infectious prose—bursting with the "attitude" she encourages her readers to embrace—Birch provides a series of guided imagery exercises. These prompts walk the reader through the nuts and bolts of learning—*imagining*—a story from the inside out in order to be fully present in its telling.

Includes notes and bibliography.

ALSO BY CAROL BIRCH
(with Melissa Heckler)

Who Says?
Essays on Pivotal Issues in Contemporary Storytelling

THE
WHOLE
STORY
HANDBOOK

*Using Imagery
to Complete the
Story Experience*

CAROL L. BIRCH

August House Publishers, Inc.
LITTLE ROCK

Published 2000 by August House Publishers, Inc.
P.O. Box 3223, Little Rock, Arkansas, 72203,
501-372-5450.

Printed in the United States of America

10 9 8 7 6 5 4 3 2 1 PB

LIBRARY OF CONGRESS CATALOGING-IN-PUBLICATION DATA
Birch, Carol (Carol L.)
    The whole story handbook : using imagery to complete the
    story experience / Carol Birch.
    p. cm.
    Includes bibliographical references.
    ISBN 0-87483-566-6 (pbk. : alk. paper)
    1. Storytelling. 2. Imagery (Psychology) I. Title.
    LB1042.B56 2000
    808.5'43—dc21   00-056604

Executive editor: Liz Parkhurst
Cover and book design: Joy Freeman

The paper used in this publication meets the minimum requirements
of the American National Standard for Information Sciences-
Permanence of Paper for Printed Library Materials, ANSI Z39.48-1984.

AUGUST HOUSE   PUBLISHERS   LITTLE ROCK

The failure of modern living is the failure of the imagination. The root meaning of the word *imagine* is "to picture to oneself." In other words, when we imagine, we create an inner picture of something not visible to our physical eye. One kind of picture we are all accustomed to is an image of something we have done or witnessed. This is the visual aspect of memory. It is not imagination. Imagination requires something more of us. It requires that we see what we have *not* seen, what we may never see, what may not even exist.

—Julius Lester, in
"Re-imagining the Possibilities,"
The Horn Book, May/June 2000

ACKNOWLEDGMENTS

The whole story is, that this book exists because of gifts given to me over a lifetime.

My family gave me a zesty, flavorful start that fed my imagination.

Students made me aware of, and taught me how to begin to articulate, the processes presented in this book.

The editors at August House made contributions large and small that improved my writing, and they continue to expand bookshelves devoted to storytelling out in the world.

Two people, in particular, enable me to relax my racing mind:

Richard Drewelus, my husband, who continues to teach me how to pause and be present to life;

Melissa Heckler, friend and writing partner, who midwifes my thoughts into books.

And finally, my appreciation goes out to the storytellers I've heard who bring words, and worlds, to life.

—Carol L. Birch

CONTENTS

INTRODUCTION

I jokingly say I tell stories because practicing the
piano was such a dreadful experience. Sitting at the
keyboard for hours was more than arduous, it was
onerous. Even if I had masterfully played a piece or two
of music, I would not have been a pianist—my heart
wasn't in it. To an unthinking public, art may be the
product, but art is *in* the work, in its creation, which is
to say—art is a process. Preparing a story for a public
event may require the same concentration of effort I
once put into playing the piano, yet, for me, the
processes of storytelling thrill and satisfy. As the saying
goes, *It's only work if you'd rather be doing something else.*

Playing music is analogous to telling a story. Music
lives when it is played, whether classical, formal forms
like symphonies or informal, fluid forms like folksongs.
Likewise, stories take on an added dimension when
shared aurally among people. As notes are played, as
words are spoken, they are transformed, adapted, and
interpreted. Even a mechanical presentation is an

interpretation; storytellers, like musicians, usually want to move far beyond the mechanical.

Restoring sound—life force, spontaneity, *chi*—to stories fixed in the silence of print is a primary pleasure and craft of storytelling. It is the focus of this book. Stories found on the page become more credible when leavened by the expressive impulses that naturally shape and color conversations with friends. Expressiveness reveals our point of view or attitudes. Stories, like conversations, thrive when attitudes are expressed about the people, places, and events within the tales. Except to underline a particular affect, we don't speak mechanically when talking about our lives, but all too often the telling of a story lacks the dynamism of a personal point of view. This book offers numerous prompts to help storytellers discover their point of view by transforming words into images with tangible, sensuous, and emotional attributes. For example, consider the differences introduced when a person is described as industrious because they are conscientious or ambitious.

Images can provoke visceral responses: think of spray-painted subway cars, walls, and fences in urban areas. Is it art or graffiti? Labeling it is one way to reveal our attitude. But *how* we say words also forcefully communicates a point of view, often more unequivocally than the choice of a word. Sneering while saying "art" or "graffiti" enables us to express the opposing view quite expressively.

Images enable us to learn stories more easily; *attitudes* help us tell them more effectively. Your responses to the prompts or questions that form the heart of this book provide an antidote to recitation and other formal presentational modes. Most importantly, your reactions to the prompts strengthen your ability to do the *one* thing that no one else is able to do—*speak with the singular authority of your own voice.*

Our attitudes reflect, embody, and express insights contributed by both the intellect and the imagination. The intellect acquires and stores data and information; the imagination stores and accesses sensations, feelings, dreams, projections, and memories. Our five senses— taste, touch, sound, sight, and smell—continually register and sort sense impressions of places, family members, friends, even strangers. Awareness resides kaleidoscopically within us. We remain largely uncon- scious of shifting shapes, sounds, and scents within, even though the impressions they make inform how we think, what we say, and how we act. Sense impressions jointly form and reveal attitudes. The ability to illumi- nate sense impressions of people and places found in stories is essential to the art of storytelling.

Just as vivid sense impressions distinguish good

writing, so does a storyteller's grasp of them support
and enlarge the telling of stories from printed sources.
Storytellers regularly learn stories from books. Virtually
all published versions of folktales are translations,
adaptations, and/or individually penned retellings.
Stories can be excerpted or adapted from novels, short
stories, poetry, biography, and history. Great stories
make what is ordinary, fresh. Stories may be long,
exquisitely wrought, and complex narratives, or they
might be what Jane Yolen calls "those tales of fantasy,
fancy, faerie, and the supra-natural, those crafted visions
and bits and pieces of dream-remembering, dreaming
that link our past and our future."[1] Layered or simple,
short or long—the best stories open us up to ourselves
and to others in profound, surprising, and refreshing
ways. As Joseph Sobol writes, stories feed our deepest
hungers: "Our psyches need stories the way our bodies
need bread to give form to our experience and to
rebuild our sense of possibility."[2]

Reading stories silently is a private act; hearing them
read is a public one. At storytelling events, however, tale
teller and tale listener are partners. Although the range
of partnership varies, the act is communal with all the
richness and echoes in that word of fellowship and
sacrament. When the collective heart skips a beat,
individuals sharing the pathos or hiccuping hilarity of

the moment find their hearts mended, minds invigorated, and spirits strengthened.

Shared stories become shared reference points, drawing people into more meaningful associations. From the deepest tenets of spiritual parables to the punchlines of jokes, stories strengthen the ties that connect families, neighbors, classmates, playmates, and co-workers with one another. Narratives provide a verbal shorthand of information, allusions, and context for future experiences.

Eleanor Farjeon's character, Elsie Piddock, is described as a "born skipper,"[3] so anyone in our family who does something very well is referred to as a born oil changer, egg decorator, tennis player, tree trimmer, dishwasher, and so forth. We use the response "Maybe...maybe not" when we want to avoid answering one another's questions—echoing the oblique response Old Hark gave Death in Richard Kennedy's story *Come Again in the Spring.*[4] Before changes large or small, my friends and I paraphrase Carl Sandburg's line that captures the disconcerting mix of hopefulness and insecurity brought by change: we know our luck is going to change but we don't know if it's good to bad or bad to good.[5] For twenty years, a friend has used a quote from the English folktale "Mr. Fox" as a mantra: "Be bold, be bold...but not too bold."[6]

In repeating these phrases, we take care to echo the tones and cadences of phrases as we originally heard them. It's the same process used in families for injunctions, proverbs, and aphorisms pronounced throughout our lives. Whether the words are from the Bible, Granny Arie, or Pooh, their stylistic suppleness preserves a distilled wisdom and affirms our relatedness.

All the same, narratives notable for a density of language may alarm potential tellers. Potent and poetic language—what Carl Sandburg called a "synthesis of hyacinths and biscuits"[7]—often attracts tellers who then feel intimidated by the material. In part such fears grow out of the belief that stories found in print must be memorized and recited in exact word order. Our reverence for the printed work is deeply felt. Literary, or print, traditions value individual ownership and alphabetic accuracy in repetition; the oral tradition recognizes community authorship, fluidity, and spontaneity. Storyteller, teacher, and scholar Melissa Heckler identifies oral tradition's principal concern as its use "as a flexible means of communication, which creates in each telling a dialogue between perceived concerns of the past, present and future."[8] Storytellers conserve elements of the past while incorporating the effects of their relationship to the text, their relationship to listeners, and the dynamics of the event itself. The conflicting

values between the two traditions must be faced by each
teller, when they tell a story found in published form.

The transposition of a story from eye to ear *is* an
adaptation of the material even when the goal is to
follow the author's lead. Some edits are quite obvious:
tag lines like "he said" and descriptors like "she spoke
boldly" become orally redundant and can usually be
dropped. Larger sections may be condensed because
descriptive material can become aurally numbing and
secondary story lines confusing. Although lines may be
repeated for emphasis as they are in conversational
speech, or a bridge may be constructed to connect one
section to another, a careful adaptation of material is
usually more a process of removing words than adding
them. If "literature is the sensuous art of causing exquisite impressions by means of words,"[9] adapting literature for oral storytelling events only enhances the
sensuous and exquisite impressions words create.
Nonetheless, every word that appears on the page
may not be used when the story is told. Storytelling is
distinct from recitation and acting. Every word becomes
a point of discovery and decision: how important is this
word to the story? for listeners? And if it is vital, how
should it be spoken?

It is imperative to examine the words an author has
chosen. What denotative and connotative meanings are

attached to the word? What images spring from it? Instead of storing word order, the next step is to store images. In 1942, Ruth Sawyer said in her seminal work, *The Way of the Storyteller:*

> I think stories must be acquired by long contempla-
> tion, by bringing the imagination to work, constantly,
> intelligently upon them. And finally by that power
> to blow the breath of life into them. And the method?
> That of learning incident by incident, or picture by
> picture. Never word by word.[10]

For half a century, storytellers have agreed on the veracity and potency of Sawyer's suggestion. Unfortunately, many storytellers do not seem to know how to translate her injunction into practice. The result is that they often tell stories with all the words in the correct order but without either the litheness of expressive language or the blood of the story flowing. The potency of the image within words projects them off the page: "sharp-tongued," "an accident of love," "knowledge dawned," "the smile ran all around the face." The list is endless. This book offers one approach for harnessing our imaginations to learn a story incident by incident, or picture by picture.

Words are the primary means of expressing images

we create in our mind's eye. Embedded in words are
cultural and personal tastes, assumptions, presupposi-
tions, and biases. Storyteller Cynthia Helms wrote about
bias in language, using an example from the Arthurian
legend of Dame Ragnel.[11] The question Arthur needed to
answer was, *What do all women desire most in the world?*
Answers in different sources vary, describing radically
different views of women.

What is crucial, and either dismissed or forgotten, is
the realization that in describing, words prescribe a
point of view. In *The Canterbury Tales,* Chaucer says
women want dominion over men.[12] In *Sir Gawain and
the Loathly Lady,* Selina Hastings' retelling asserts "What
women most desire is to have their own way."[13] Storyteller Heather Forest chooses the words "their own
sovereignty—the right to rule themselves, to do with
their lives as they wish" (and adds a thoughtful aside
from King Arthur, who says: "I would want no less for
myself").[14] Even this abbreviated comparison of author-
ial choices clarifies the way each and every word shapes
and shades a story.

The ability to imagine is richer than merely visualiz-
ing the story. Seeing with the inward eye is only one
form of imaging. Equating images in stories primarily
with visual orientation is a conditioned bias. Those
blind from birth have the capacity to imagine. With its

root in image—and with related terms like visualization, picture, reflection, mirror, the mind's eye, second sight, etc.—the notion of imagination narrows almost exclusively to the visual in our dominant mall culture. All cultures are not visually oriented. Inuits, for example, are more oriented around sound because an overwhelming darkness on one hand or the glare from snow on the other can blur or erase visual cues.

Limiting images and the imagination to visual acuity is attractive in a cerebral age. It lends itself to a kind of purity: no embarrassing or jarring noises, no sweat, no odors, no gluttony, no libidinous sensuality. Ask someone to smell their way through a story and responses may include giggles, suspicions, or revulsion. Yet, just as full sensory awareness enriches daily life, sensory awareness makes characters and settings vivid and compelling.

Using the imagination to make character and setting more substantial is offered as a technique to abolish more studied techniques for manipulating voice, face, and body. More focused use of the powers of the imagination may better serve the transposition of a story from page to aurally expressive language. Accessing the imagination is relatively simple, compared to studying a variety of techniques for public performance. Imaginative insights also personalize a story. Re-imaging a story doesn't make it yours in any legal or ethical sense, but more personal associations with a story bring unique qualities of your energy and voice to the work. This is comparable to a song being interpreted by musicians—the differences can be quite remarkable, giving performers their signature style. The signature style may define an artist, but it develops in the process of doing the work and may evolve over time.

To make a story compelling, it is *not* necessary to have been present when events occurred. What matters is *at the time of the telling, we are fully present.* "Seeing" is the first step. We see; then we assess. Assessment clarifies our attitude—about the place, the people, and what happened. When we are engaged, our adrenaline is pumping. This process is revealed in our expressive attitudes. These expressive attitudes give stories juice. Any storyteller who has not considered the cruel condescension of Mr. Fox, in the English folktale of the same name, cannot convincingly bring him to life, let alone communicate horror at his actions. In speech, these attitudes become obvious through chosen words, vocal tones, facial expressions, and other body language. The proverbial "It's not what you say, it's how you say it" is a primary source of the storyteller's effectiveness.

A startling example of this was mentioned in a book review in *The New York Times*. Brian Heap, a storyteller

in Jamaica, held a workshop for young people and read
a news item about bullying with two very different
attitudes. The first time, he read belligerently, roaring
above a tape of raucous music so that the adolescents—
including the girls—raised their fists and cheered for the
bully. The next time he read it softly and sympatheti-
cally with quiet piano music in the background. Students became subdued, and one or two cried.[15]

If you're not engaged, how can your audience become
viscerally involved? I heard a report on National Public
Radio on a study of memory. The question they were
seeking to answer was: why, after terrible experiences,
do people report that images of horror repeatedly flash
through their minds? Scientists determined there are
links between adrenaline and memory. Two groups were
shown the same film. Participants were led to believe
the film depicted an accident that had actually occurred.
One group was given adrenaline suppressants; the other
group was not. Two months later, the subjects whose
adrenaline had been suppressed remembered almost
nothing. Members of the other group spoke with an
array of amazingly precise and vivid details.

Storytelling is most interesting when the storyteller is
not acting out a part, but rather doing *two* things simultaneously. Through verbal *and* nonverbal clues, effective
storytellers bring out the nuances, both large and small,

which delineate characters within the story and direct the point of view of an audience toward the characters. Actors may use sense memory to bring a character to life, but they submerge their own *selves* in service of character. Storytellers are not hidden. Not only are they present, they communicate their love, approval, compassion, contempt, fear, or other direct judgements of, and responses to, the characters in a story.

Creating and juggling such fluid and layered realities may sound daunting, but we actively engage in it every day. When friends gossip, commiserate, or recreate the dialogues of their favorite soap opera characters, they freely communicate their approval and disapproval at the latest turn of events. At home when we recount the day's adventures or the treasured stories of our family's shared past, most of our characterizations share a narrative duality—*simultaneously repeating what a person said while commenting on them.* Generally speaking, imitations of the beloved and hated figures of our lives include judgmental overtones. We don't imitate them dispassionately. We communicate attitudes about them, so listeners grasp the full import of the personalities involved—our own personalities *and* the person being described. Friends may encourage us with "Yes, that's him! He's such a stitch, nerd, gentleman, creep"—fill in the blank. Or they may object to or try to balance a biased portrait: "Don't be so hard on her. You took what she said all wrong."[16]

No one needs to take a class or read a book to learn how to say "I love you" to someone they adore. Without acting or public speaking courses, people reflexively and expressively use their voices, faces, and bodies, to express attitudes all the time. Capitalizing on this innate ability moves storytelling from monotoned deliveries, from a "let's pretend" sugary superficiality, and from the artificially mellifluous and insincere intonations of radio and television non-personalities. Each day we speak effortlessly with a diverse array of attitudes that are naturally compelling.

If you need to be convinced of the scope of your talents, put a tape recorder by your telephone. Tape only your half of your telephone conversations for a month. You will hear how spontaneously and expressively attitudes fly out of your mouth. You may also be stunned by the number and variety of attitudes you readily possess and express. I witnessed a dramatic example in class when I suggested students tape their responses to those irksome telephone solicitations. Suddenly boisterous accounts erupted on all sides. Previously quite contained students vied with one another to tell their stories. Believe me, attitudes flew.

Like storytelling workshops, books on storytelling

are generally useful in that they remind us of what we
already know. I hope this book greases the hinges of the
doors into your storehouse of knowledge, experience,
insight, and imagination. The prompts will help stir up
the resourcefulness of your imagination, which contains
unforgettable details—textures, tastes, sights, smells,
sounds, and a vivid array of emotions.

This book is a call for you to ground stories in all of
your senses. Our senses pose and answer questions: *How
does a character look and sound? What does the food taste
and smell like? What is the weather?* It is a call to bring all
of your senses and sensibilities to bear on stories,
whether you are recreating written texts for oral storytelling events, assisting others in understanding dimensions of character and setting, or writing original
material.

An enormous number of questions fill this book. *Not
all of them will be helpful.* Remember, the questions are
offered as prompts, not a prescribed path. You do not
have to labor at answering every question for each story.

LOOK AGAIN

*To find the whole story, we must sometimes return to
the story many times. As an exercise, look closely
at the art used for the front cover of this book.
Is there more there than you first perceived?*

In different stories, different questions become primary. One or more prompts may even lead to unexpected or vitalizing insights. I offer the extensive questions because people look at things so differently. The imagination's understanding is qualitatively different from information provided by cultural or scholarly research. The senses and imagination do not replace research; they are intended to complement it. The imagination can humanize research—put a pulse to it and leave a footprint, a scent, a memory behind.

WORKING WITH TEXTS

Once, as a community liaison librarian, I visited a preschool because the teachers contended their children did not like stories—a first, if true. When I arrived, though, it became readily apparent why the children could not focus their attention on stories. One contributing factor to the problem was the schedule for story times. Teachers read when children were waiting to be picked up at the end of the day. Truth is stranger than fiction, and the story read was as disjointed as the following:

Once upon a time...

> *DAVID, your father's here. Mr. Smith, please bring David's milk money tomorrow; he forgot it again today...*

There was a beautiful princess...

> *Keisha, honey, your mother's here—pick up dolly, Keisha. Good girl...*

The princess awoke one day...

The other time the teachers read to the children was when inclement weather kept everyone inside during recess. At the time of day when the preschoolers expected to be most active, they were suddenly expected to be especially quiet and attentive. These poor decisions pale in comparison to what came next.

The teacher read *Millions of Cats* by Wanda Gag. That she read it dully, without intonation, was only a hint of what was to come. The story has a very rhythmic and satisfying refrain: "There were hundreds of cats, thousands of cats, millions and billions and trillions of cats."[1] The first time these words appeared in the text, she read them. The next time they appeared, she actually said: "There were hundreds of cats, et cetera."

Et cetera! The children looked at the woman as if she had grabbed candy from them. And well she had! In a fundamental way, her reading robbed the story of sweetness, music, and power.

Before damning the teacher too righteously, we have to ask ourselves if we don't do the same thing when we silently read through a collection in our search for a story to tell—especially stories that include a great deal of repetition. We do have a tendency to skip refrains, repetitive lines, even parallel segments. "Oh, that again," we say dismissively as we hurry on. Intrinsically, we miss a vital part of the message when we ignore cumulative or repetitive sections of a story. In such instances, the medium *is* a crucial component of the message.

In searching for stories to tell, I suggest you read— nearly everything—aloud. In the short run, this takes a long time; in the long run, it reduces the search for tellable stories. When we read aloud, we physically *feel* the writer's style and phrasing—if it is easy, exhilarating, or disjointed. We *hear* qualities in the language as we sound out words. "Talk about mean!" is the explosive opening to Truman Capote's *The Thanksgiving Visitor.*[2] The words are colloquial, expressive, internally ener- getic—and they draw us right into the story.

Seemingly common openings: "Once upon a time there was a beautiful princess named Rosemary"—can seem bland when glossed over silently. But when read with expression, the sentence suddenly alerts us to the astonishing information in Laurence Houseman's story, "The Wooing of the Maze," that[3]:

ONCE-upon-a-time, there WAS

a *Beautiful Princess*

...named *Rosemary*

Reading books aloud becomes a daunting task when we are faced with pressures to find a story for the program

tomorrow, next week, next month. We often face hor-
rific time and "theme" story-hour limitations. Nonetheless, if the goal is to find stories to tell for a lifetime,
reading aloud is a shortcut. If a story lingers in the
mind, if it delights or intrigues, photo-copy the story
and keep it on file to work with immediately or to look
at again weeks, months, or years later.

There is no single or "correct" way to learn a story. I
offer a flexible approach that has served me well. When
it is finally time to focus on a story, read it aloud once a
day over one or many weeks. After seven to ten readings
stretched out over weeks, it is amazing how fully we
come to understand the characters and the sequence of
events. At that point, close the book and retell the story
in your own words.

This rough telling is concerned with identifying
characters, major problems they face, important scenes,
and the forward pitch of events. Identify all the people
and scenes that would be painted if the story appeared
as a mural on a wall—a mural, not a storyboard. Beginning storytellers tend to focus far too much attention on
exact sequence, the restrictive nature of storyboards.
Murals remind us of the simultaneity of life. Each
moment is more than inextricably part of what came
before and what happens next; it exists concurrently in
time and memory.

When the mural exists within the mind's eye, the prompts that follow begin to transform it into a three dimensional world. Originally, I worked from an audio-tape of the questions and rigorously set aside time to answer them, following the exercises with eyes closed. Now I consider the prompts less formally, making time for discoveries to surface through quiet reverie. This more contemplative form of thought takes longer. I may be sitting, but more often I am washing dishes, dusting, ironing, rearranging things, or walking. My house is never so clean as when I am mentally moving images around in my head!

Each character, every important scene, details of setting—these are pieces that fit together and create something larger than the sum of their parts, like a puzzle. So, on a given day, break off a piece of the puzzle and carry it around like a key or a talisman for a time. Metaphorically, turn it around to see which way the pattern goes. Learn its edges. Sometimes keep it as a focal point; sometimes let it float on the fringe of consciousness. Whether you are formally focusing or informally considering characters and setting, both can be useful. It is up to you to discover which best serves your style and schedule.

Check the text, but remember, what matters is *knowing more than appears on the page*. Stories are full

of lines like: "Then the king walked into the room." All
too often, this type of narrative line receives no expressive consideration and is delivered with no perceivable
attitude. In contrast to tossing out such a common
narrative line, the delivery of this line is as important
and potent as any line of dialogue. Students of storytelling regularly struggle with the dynamics of sound to
make dialogue authentic. Narrative lines deserve the
same diligent care. Actor Kathy Bates said, during her
interview on the program *Inside the Actor's Studio*, that
she wants a director to let her know he's been where
he's asking her to go, and he's waiting for her when she
turns the corner.[4] In this sense, storytellers function as
directors.

When a storyteller speaks the line, "Then the king
walked into the room," s/he needs to know:

How is he walking?

How does he feel as he approaches the room:
eager/dreading, tentative/assured, happy/sorrowful,
calm/angry, or some combination of feelings?

What room is he entering?
Public or private room?
Where is this room in relation to other rooms?

The normal domain for royalty or servants?
A room he'll dwarf or be dwarfed by?

What does he expect to find in the room?

What does he think will happen?

What will fulfill or thwart his expectations?

How do you, as the storyteller/narrator, feel about him?

How do you feel about what will happen to him in this room?

Suddenly, the line "Then the king walked into the room," is a whole scene in and of itself. A line that was tossed aside and colorless now has colors and a pulse. The storyteller's inner vision is like a camera panning the scene of the king entering a room. The mind, like a movie, projects the passage of time, the movement of shapes, hues, textures, and sound effects. Because storytelling evokes full sensory awareness, there are scents in the air and responses to temperature and clothing, as well as perceptions of the bitterness or joy lingering in the mouth of the king.

Knowing only the words as rote memorization is

comparable to walking a tightrope through a story. Tightrope walking must be thrilling to do; it is certainly exhilarating to *see* the singular control and acrobatic skill of performers. In the long run though, this may not be the most productive metaphor for the relationship of the storyteller to the story or to the audience. Too breathless. Too performance oriented. The focus is the walker's skill; the relationship between artist and audience is skewed by a heightened awareness of the void between them; part of the attraction comes from the tension created at watching someone dare death. Above all, storytelling is about relationship, not performing with an audience sitting tensely below. People sometimes talk about storytelling as if it were climbing Mt. Everest: it requires a great deal of equipment, an uphill course, a precipitous climb—and few people ever succeed. Both metaphors are at odds with feeling grounded and related.

When a story is deeply internalized, it becomes such familiar territory that the storyteller can take a detour, knows which side roads are worth traveling down, and what vistas lie ahead. Genuine familiarity allows us to confidently invite others to travel with us. Being well-prepared, our focus can be on enjoying the journey *with our listeners*.

The most important qualities shared among great

storytellers are that they remain true to themselves and true to their own style. They are present. They are natural while possessing great depth of feeling for stories and listeners. Their enthusiasm is contagious and affects listeners. This does not mean each story sounds bright or jolly. Rather, a vitality supports the more fleeting qualities of engagement like joy, alarm, or concern for whatever is happening in the story. Focused energy says the storyteller cares about the people, places, and events in the story as it unfolds.

All stories should not sound the same, and within stories, a storyteller's voice does not remain the same. The range of the voice creates differences that shade and shape a tale. Mice need not speak unendingly in squeaky voices. Mice could squeak, because playfulness is as grounding as more serious approaches, but story-tellers need not be restricted to such artifice. When a story is grounded in actual experience—the confronta-tion between someone who is vulnerable (mouse) with someone who is larger and stronger (cat)—much more latitude of expression is possible. The goal is to commu-nicate the two distinct personalities and some dimen-sion of the struggle between them, to not sound *unintentionally* affected. The storyteller's cleverness serves the story, not the reverse. The range between the extremes of ham-actor and human tape recorder is vast.

Five problems are heard repeatedly at storytelling events. As storytellers gain experience, the problems become more subtle. All too often tellers:

- are not prepared;
- recite words without seeming to understand what they are saying;
- speak with artificially mellifluous language that bears no relation to the meaning of the words;
- tell story after story with the same expressive language, pace, and cadence, so that a regal myth sounds just like a gossipy anecdote—in short, all of the stories sound alike, no care has been taken to work with varieties of tone in the tales;
- develop a shtick—so every kid, old man, etc.— sounds the same in story after story. (This can be appealing if you hear one story, but not in a succession of tales.)

If dealt with thoughtfully, the prompts offered will help minimize, or eradicate, these kinds of problems.

- As storytellers, we will be *well* prepared.
- We are better able to tell a story in an associative, oral way rather than as recitation.

- The problem of artificially mellifluous language is eradicated when fictional characters and places become real.

- When using information gleaned from the prompts for working with and understanding a text, the dangers of distorting it are minimized.

- Finally, when characters have a full-sensory presence with sound, sight, scent, taste, and texture, each kid and old man will have so much substance that talking about them as if they were the same will be as foreign as talking about two relatives as if they were the same.

CHARACTER

In our family, Nunny is what we call our grandmothers. My father's mother lives on in my memory as a slight woman with a half-smile, wearing a thin sweater over a housedress faded from repeated washing. Her slippered, swollen feet tap rhythmically to songs sung under her breath. The kitchen where she sits seems perpetually warmed and fragrant from stews in the oven and soups simmering on the stove. Her hand rests on the yellowed and cracked oilcloth, which covers a small table next to a window. The back lighting from the window transforms her hair into a halo of white around her wrinkled face—a soft-toned, mythic grandmother.

In contrast, Nunny for my niece is my mother. When asked about *her* grandmother, she would describe a spirited, slim, ninety-year-old grandmother with hair permed and coiffed. Her Nunny smiles broadly in her sequined, green satin evening suit, her earrings swinging wildly, as she dances every dance at a recent family wedding.

Images of grandmothers are as varied as the women themselves, yet all too often storytellers regularly indicate fictional elderly women by adding a quality of wobbliness to their speech or bearing. Living in the midst of four thousand senior citizens, I see many elderly women like my mother, definite in speech and sure on their feet. More women seem to walk erect than are crippled by osteoporosis. To be sure, some women do struggle and stumble through the grocery store; nonetheless, others prowl or march—and a few glide. Not all elderly women move like geriatric beetles.

Consciously or unconsciously—on some level—we grasp the characteristics which identify the people in our daily lives. We are not confused when telling stories about the differences and similarities of two bachelor uncles. Our faces, voices, and bodies communicate a thousand things about them and our relationship with each of them. In the mind's eye, their individuality exists as an amalgamation of sense impressions that inform everything we say about them. These impressions

CONSIDER

Take a moment to consider the kaleidoscopic images, sense impressions, and memories that come when you think—Grandmother or Uncle.

Now sharpen the focus on one image and describe as many details as you are able.

are the basis of our attitudes about them.

With fictional characters, though, we need to *discover* their presence and our responses to them in order to talk about them with the same compelling conviction. Unfortunately, when people tell stories from printed sources, they forget what they know in life—that zillions of traits make up character and distinguish us from one another. We only have to look to begin to discover what they are. All too often, fictional characters are described generically or limited by stereotypes. Students respond to a request to describe a boy in a story with: "He's a typical eight-year-old boy." What *is* a typical eight-year-old boy? Stand in the middle of a classroom full of eight-year-old boys, and differences are readily apparent in height, weight, ethnicity, clothing, hair-styling, cleanliness, carriage, demeanor, etc. From such visual clues, people make all kinds of assessments about a given boy's personality, academic record, self-confidence, level of physical activity, and economic status. If the boys speak, or change locations or eras, such differences increase exponentially.

We have to beware of a latent (or overt) narrow-mindedness behind remarks like, "They all look alike." At best such *thought*-less dismissal has a stultifying effect on a story; at worst it results in caricatures and stereo-types—making a story boring or offensive. The more

individuated a character is for us, the more likely it is
that we will introduce characters who come to life for
our listeners.

First we "see" characters' physical characteristics and
then we assess what we see to make decisions about
their personalities and character; this tends to be a
rather automatic and unconscious process. This all-too-
human tendency gives first impressions great impact.
Cynthia De Felice's novel, *Lostman's River*, clearly demonstrates this process without pejorative overtones. A boy,
in 1906, sees a stranger poling a canoe up to his landing
on a river in Florida:

> Quickly, without staring, I took in the details of the
> man's appearance. He was dressed commonly enough,
> in shirt, hat, trousers, and galluses, but his clothes
> were a lot cleaner than those of most folks who came
> up the river. He didn't have the hard look of the
> plume hunter, who came shooting birds for their
> fancy feathers, or the smell of gator skinners, who
> killed crocodiles and alligators for their hides. He
> didn't act shifty and jumpy, the way the moonshiners
> did, most of 'em half crazy from drinking the liquor
> they made to sell. He wasn't a Seminole Indian or a
> black man, either. So what was he doing poling way
> up Lostman's River to where we'd made our home?[1]

In this short passage we learn a great deal about the stranger—and the boy. Although the man is a stranger, his clothing is not strange; only his cleanliness is remarkable. Otherwise, his appearance lacks distinguishing characteristics of great wealth or poverty, personal flamboyance, and cultural or racial characteristics attributed to Native and African Americans by the boy. The stranger is not outfitted for familiar types of local employment. He is sober and calm in his bearing; his demeanor doesn't project callousness; and finally, because he is clean and does not reek of slaughtering or liquor, he may be a step up socially from those employed in more coarse or illegal endeavors.

In life we "read" people like this all the time. The primary goal of this section of the book is to engage you in a similar process with characters in stories you tell. It literally brings characters to life when you give them a dimension beyond stick figures or the stereotypes of central casting.

ALL IN THE ATTITUDE

Consider the options for Death, who as a character in a story, says: "Come with me." If Death is described as "the envious one who grins and licks his lips at the prospect of going after someone's soul with a bitter sword and cape of hate, envy and rage,"[2] *the depth of our repulsion would affect how we deliver his lines.*

Contrast such a delivery with the options in the story "Death and the Red-Headed Woman."[3] The title itself indicates that something much less malevolent and more lively is about to occur. The story centers on the longing both Death and the Red-Headed Woman have for a mate. Since the entirely winsome and spirited Red-Headed Woman chooses Death for her mate, we can be confident of his innate goodness. Death in this story is not ancient or diabolical; he is a mature, compassionate, and lonely man who leads people from one reality to another.

Seeing Death in a radically different light changes how he might say: "Come with me." *The depth of our feeling for him changes how we say what he said.* When we have strong attitudes about people, it is almost impossible to hide them.

In life our attitudes give us away all the time. Years ago, for example, neighbors to the right and left of us were elderly women named Mary. In just a simple introduction, it would be obvious which of them I adored— *even while I was being polite to the other.* My eyes, jaw, and general body posture would relax when introducing the retired librarian whose gentleness and dignity were so appealing. The other Mary was cruel and paranoid. Although politeness would have masked other feelings, the *contrast* in my manner around these two women would reveal truer feelings for each of them.

Likewise, consider telephone conversations we've overheard. When the people with whom we live or work answer the phone in our presence, we frequently know to whom they are speaking—by their audible (even inaudible) sigh, their intonation, word, shift of the shoulders. Their nonverbal cues such as tone of voice and body language communicate their reactions quite instantaneously and most effectively.

THE FROG PRINCE: A CASE STUDY

In stories, our attitudes have a great deal of leeway because characters often mature quite rapidly. Stories compress and encapsulate time. In the well-known story "The Frog Prince," for example, the girl matures rapidly. At the opening of the tale, she is a self-absorbed pre-schooler. Her wrists are delectably sweet with chubby baby creases as she rolls a golden ball on the ground. When she asks the frog to get the ball, she's too young to grasp the full import of the bargain she's made. In the next important scene with her father, when the frog has come to the door, she has matured sufficiently to knowingly protest her innocence in the face of her guilt. At this point, she is reminiscent of an eight year old who tries to distract parents from the truth with too literal, legalistic arguments over irrelevant issues. When the princess feeds the frog from her plate, she is a grossed out middle-schooler. When she throws the frog against the wall, she is a young teenager savvy enough to refuse unwanted sexual advances. By the time she chooses to sleep with the prince and when she emerges from their bedchamber the next morning, she is a young woman and bride of nineteen.

The prompts that follow brought the character of the princess to life for me. They are offered as an example, not to limit options in retelling this story. Through all the changes, what remains constant in my mind is the shimmer of the air around her, electric with golden rays. The rays reflect from and back to her hair even as it grows longer, as well as from the shine of silken dresses. These rays also explode around her in bursts of temper and laughter. Her wrists grow thinner and more delicate in each scene. The princess is willful from start to finish, but she moves from the natural self-centeredness of a child to a young woman's loving maturity in an extremely brief time. Would I enumerate any of these specific images? Nintey-nine percent of the time—no. These images just make her more concrete, more human, for me to talk about someone I see with conviction.

Could the tone of the story change? Yes, because

feelings toward willful girls change. Sometimes girls
whose willfulness seems to express an overwhelming
sense of entitlement are exasperating. Other times such
behavior strikes us as a childish bravado ineffectively
trying to mask vulnerability. Another time we might cheer,
seeing her willfulness as boldness, and celebrate her
refusal to be controlled. A storyteller's mood changes—
or the audiences' responses establish a different tone—
and attitudes toward the behavior of characters shift.
These alterations color the subtext of the story, but the
core of the story doesn't change. The growth and maturity
of the princess is tangible, admirable, and appropriate.

Similarly, the ending can be shaded with a wide
spectrum of color. The stance toward the princess at the
end of the folktale could be one of a proud parent:
"That's my daughter for you! She's always known her
mind and nothing will ever stop her." The mood could
easily be less parental, more impersonal. We are sometimes tender, awestruck by love's continued power to
transform lives. Or we shake our heads: "Kids! She's so
young and so blinded by love. I'm worried—a little, a
great deal, scared witless—she acted too fast!" Friends
talk about new marriages from a thousand different
perspectives, and we can tell stories with just as many
moods. Shades in mood are like lighting in film; they
provide a variety of effects.

DANGEROUS CURVE AHEAD

A word of caution: don't go overboard when assessing a character. Beware of projecting psychological battle scars onto evil, nasty, and unpleasant characters. Unlike life, most characters in traditional tales are either good or bad, devoid of the more realistic ambiguities that unsettle our psyches and souls. The hero arouses our sympathies and encourages us all by prevailing in the face of prodigious difficulties. The fabulous forces of stupidity and evil arouse our antipathies, and we feel vindicated in seeing them overcome. Folk literature is spare, and traits are often externalized. It ruins the inherent balance in a story to bring post-Freudian psychological projections to bear on the witch's troubled childhood. People can get caught up in waxing eloquent and pouring meaningful insights into the slender neck of one of history's most compact vessels.

If our feelings toward a character are sympathetic, any indications of dental problems might increase our sympathy for them. "Oh, did you see his teeth? I'll bet he's had trouble getting proper care all his life. He's probably had terrible toothaches, etc." If, on the other hand, we dislike the character, we could easily say: "Oh, did you see his teeth? Gross! I'll bet he's had bad breath all his life. Imagine kissing him—yuck!"

Not everyone recoils from an angry face nor advances to comfort those in sorrow. A friend, whose daughter was killed in an automobile accident, once told me she has been amazed at how people distance themselves from her and her sorrow. Some avoid her outright; others go to great lengths to avoid any mention of the accident in which the girl died; others make no inquiries— sympathetic or curious—about how this friend might be processing her feelings. People not only do not mention her daughter, they do not speak to her about her other children or even what their own children are doing.

A petite friend with quite a childlike face has a great deal of trouble having her anger taken seriously. The old line—"You look so cute when you're angry"—is her reality, and she hates it. People step right toward her when she's angry; because she looks so childlike and vulnerable, they assume she needs comforting.

The prompts are offered to trigger tangible *impressions* with periodic close-ups that bring a character startlingly to life. As you move through the questions, beware of over-reading, over-psychologizing, overdoing it with a heavy hand—period. This warning, followed by so many detailed questions, may seem paradoxical. It is.

The initial prompts address details of a character's physical appearance. Although not all prompts lead to big discoveries, they add physical weight to ethereal characters and make an emotional response to them more probable. Ray Bradbury is a master at revealing details that bring characters to life: "The day Joe Pipkin was born all the Orange Crush and Nehi soda bottles in the world fizzed over...His great round face burned with fresh sun. His eyes flashed Morse code signals."[4] Instantly we see a boy's infectious and uncontainable exuberance, his extraordinarily expressive eyes, and a round face that mirrors the brilliance of the sun. Contrast Pipkin's eyes to these: eyes that open slow as a frog, eyes acknowledging satisfaction, eyes dulled by pain, eyes lit with wooing.

In becoming more aware of physical details, we become aware of other stories in the life of a character. Take, for example, this subsequent Bradbury passage:

[Pipkin's] tennis shoes were ancient. They were colored green of forests jogged through, brown from old harvest trudged through September a year back, tar-stained from sprints along the docks and beaches where the coal barges came in, yellow from careless dogs, splinter-filled from climbing wood fences...His hands, mittened with dust and the good smell of airedales and peppermint and stolen peaches from the far country orchards.[5]

Suddenly, the forests, harvests, docks, beaches, dogs, splinters, dirt, and orchards around Pipkin all become episodes to possibly consider and savor. Details bring Pipkin to life; they lead to other avenues for discoveries; they provide readers or listeners with evocative images to which to respond. In talking about his process of writing, Bradbury models a journey similar to ones the prompts suggest. He sends himself back in the past with words as catalysts and learns to allow his senses to tell him all that is true:

> I floundered into a word-association process in which I simply got out of bed each morning, walked to my desk, and put down any word or series of words that happened along in my head. *Thus I fell into surprise*…Once I learned to keep going back I had plenty of memories and sense impressions to play with, not work with, no, play with.[6] [italics added]

This is your invitation to fall into surprise. This is the time to consider: how do you know what you know about the characters in your story? The author provides the clues, but everyone who comes in contact with a character perceives that person uniquely. The paradox is that we pull back from what we thought we knew, to make a more objective assessment of *who a character is*, so we can finally speak more subjectively. In the end, our engagement with a character draws an audience into a closer relationship with us and with the character also.

It is a *process*, not to be forced; it is a process of trial and error. Please allow yourself to change your mind—repeatedly. Try on. Discard. Above all, play.

CHARACTER PROMPTS

Imagine a character standing and facing you, so you
easily see her from head to foot. Notice:

Height

Weight

Proportions of

Head

Torso (neck, shoulders, chest, waist, stomach, hips)

Arms and legs

Hands and feet

Is anything in her stance indicative of her personality?

Shyness/Forthrightness

Self-Confidence/Insecurity

Warmth/Coolness

Agitation/Calmness

To a great extent, clothing is a response to the natural environment and social world in which a person lives. What we choose to wear and how we wear it also expresses personality. A character's clothing can tell us about the following:

Physical features of environment

Climate

Season

Weather

Time of day

Social Constraints

> Era

> Status

> Wealth

> Is the character dressed for work, recreation, religious observance?

From looking at the attire, would you say this person unconsciously got dressed, or did they consciously "dress" in the morning?

What decorative elements are visible in her appearance?

> Jewelry

> Piercings

> Painting/Tattoos

Does anything about her clothing restrict her movement?

How she stands?

Sits?

Moves?

Just as you noticed the general proportions of the body, as you walk closer, notice how her head and face are proportioned:

Size and shape of the head, forehead, cheekbones, eyes, nose, mouth, chin, jaw, ears

Is it balanced?

What is pleasing?

What is remarkable?

Look at the skin on the face:

> Color

> Complexion

> Texture: smoothness, scars, finely lined or creased from frowning, squinting, or smiling

> Tone, especially eyelids and jawline

Eyes:

> Color

> Shape

> Distance between the eyes

> How deeply set are they?

> How are they shaped?

> Are the outer corners of her eyes higher than, even with, or lower than the inner corners?

The muscles around the eyes reveal most about a character. Some people literally look at the world wide-eyed, while others narrow their vision. For most people the two sides of the face are very different indeed, one far more open or alert than the other.

Does the character look happy?

What other word would be more precise?

How does this character look at the world?

How much tension is apparent around her eyes?

How expressive are the eyes?

Are differences in the two eyes subtle or not?

Does the character see clearly?

Does she distort her face to see better?

Wear any kind of corrective lenses?

Look at the mouth. Does the mouth relax into a Mona Lisa smile, a straight line, or a frown?

How much tension is apparent in her jaw?

When you consider the following emotions, see which of them play over the character's face readily, slightly, fleetingly, or not at all:

Fear

Anger

Joy

Sorrow

Love

Repeat the emotions and notice how the feeling was made evident. Which muscles moved?

If you extend your hands with the palms up, imagine the palms of the character's hands resting on yours.

How do her hands feel?
Heavy/Light

Dry/Damp

Smooth/Rough

How large are her hands?

Does she have any rings on her fingers?

Does she have any scars anywhere on her hands?

Look at the backs of her hands:

Shape and length of fingers

Shape and length of nails

Care of nails and cuticles

Turn over her hands.

When you look at her palms, what do you notice?

What assumptions can you make about this person's life, based on her hands?

How much manual labor has she done?

How pampered has she been?

What care does she take of them?

In the end, what is most noticeable about her hands?

Let go of her hands and look down at her feet:

What, if anything, is she wearing on her feet?

How are the shoes fastened:
woven straps, ties, buckles, Velcro?

What material are they made of?

How stylish are the shoes?

How comfortable are the shoes?

How well are they cared for?

Are they polished?

Worn down on the heels? soles?

As the character continues to face forward, slowly step around to look at her profile.

How does she stand?

Rigid/Relaxed

Erect/Slouched

Is her body in basic alignment?

If out of alignment, which part is thrust forward—the head, shoulders, hips, or feet?

Is anything obvious from the side that you missed looking straight at her?

As you continue walking behind the character, how are the hips and shoulders proportioned?

From the back, take a closer look at the character's hair:

Color

Texture

Body

Cleanliness/Shine

Styling

A person may take great care fixing the hair around the face, but is the back of it a mess?

Continue walking around the character. Is one profile remarkable in any way from the other?

What odors or scents emanate from the character?

How pleasant are these smells?

Do they relate to work or play?

As you face the character again, imagine you can see an aura of energy about her. What kind of energy does she give off?

Some people are calm and cool; others are calm and warm. Some people radiate anger that is like dry ice—so cold it burns; another's anger is explosive but short-lived, like dry kindling; anger in others smolders for unbelievably long periods of time. The energy contained in—and radiating out from—love, joy, fear, anger, and sorrow can be just as dramatic. These five emotions are not the only ones, but they are the primary ones.

Which of those primary emotions dominate and energize this character, even in repose?

If you ask the character to walk with you, how does she walk?

Head, shoulders, hips, or feet first?

How large are her steps?

How graceful are her movements?

How fast does she walk?

Where does she look while walking?

How would you describe how this person walks through life?

How willing is she to dance?

What kind of dancing does she do?

How well does she dance?

If you ask a question and the character answers, what qualities do you hear?

Rate at which she speaks

Pitch

Volume

Tone

How comfortable is she when talking?

How much silence is in her speech?

How comfortable is she with silence?

How comfortable is she with singing?

How well does she sing?

The next series of questions focuses on a character *in a setting*. The same prompts could be used for different settings in the story. Imagine walking with a character as he enters a building or room in the story:

Does the character pause before entering? Why?

How carefully does the character enter the space?

Does he seem to fill or be dwarfed by the space?

Does he dominate or fit in with the other characters in the space?

Does he seem comfortable in this place?

What is the first thing he does?

What does he seem to value here?

What follows are more general questions about the character's role and growth in the story and his relationships with others.

Is the character a seeker or a victim at the beginning of the story?

Does this change during the course of the story?

What goals does the character have?

Do these goals change during the story?

What has the character gained by the end?

How has the character dealt with obstacles along the way?

Which traits have been most balanced? Most imbalanced?

Courage

Compassion

Sense of humor

Common sense

Love

What does the character say about himself?

Is he reliable?

How do you know this?

What are his best characteristics?

What are his weaknesses?

Does he have special talents?

What is his relationship with others in the tale?

A character's speech can reveal the relationship between himself and the person to whom he is speaking.

> How does this character speak to the other characters in the story?

> What do we know about him from this behavior?

Whom does this character love?

> How do his actions convey support and care for those he loves?

What do others say about the character?

Are they reliable?

How do you know this?

Think of ways in which the character is the same as others in the story.

In what important ways is he different?

How would he argue with another character, using words, sounds, and space?

How would he express his affection for another character, using words, sounds, and space?

How do relationships alter between this character and others during the story?

Visualize how the character would stand in proximity to all the other characters in the story.

When the story begins

During the height of the action in the middle of the story

By the end of the story

SETTING

"Once upon a time" is all times. "In a faraway king-
dom" is all realms. Innumerable tales, especially those
adapted for children from European cultures, begin
with these invocations of universality. Many more tales
begin with universal references to more ancient and
diverse cultures, "When animals could talk..." or "This
is what the old ones say..." All of these ritual invocations invite teller and listener to relax into the dreamlike
realm of story. The conscious mind is invited to give up
linear processes so that the unconscious can freely make
associative connections.

As storytellers, however, we cannot be lulled into
thinking that the realm of story is a bland, nonspecific,
unrooted, artificial world. Firmly attached to times,
people, places, and things, stories brilliantly display the
details of their physical and cultural origins, celebrating
time and place.

People tend to think of setting explicitly. Time and
place consitute more than the names of locales and

years alluded to. Setting is absolutely, implicitly embedded in stories. Choices in food, clothing, flora, fauna, *building materials, building styles, government and* class structures—all reveal era and locale. What people say and how they say it reveals setting. We recognize this easily in foreign languages: where the Japanese say "konichiwa" in greeting, the Ju/'hoan say "/xai-o." Change eras and the "thou" of the King James Bible becomes "you" in contemporary usage. Between regions of the United States colloquial speech varies, as Northerners say "hi" while "hey" is used in Southern states.

The way implicit differences are imbedded in language may be more complicated or culturally relevant. In the Irish language, no single words mirror English's "yes" and "no." Subject and verb are repeated. "It is" or "it is not" may be used or shortened to " 'tis" and " 'tis not." In answering questions, the verb is repeated: "Would you?" "I would." "Can we go?" "We can." These examples underscore the aural alertness and affirming nature of conversation in Ireland. As one of my students pointed out, he would have to pay much closer attention to what his wife said if he were going to answer this way.

The king in Norwegian folktales may well relax in his kitchen, even open the door to visitors himself; no Japanese emperor ever would. The power of the sea affects storylines from around the world. The icy waters

over which a fur-clad Inuit paddles in a kayak offer
dramatic possibilities that both overlap and differ from
the balmy water over which a nearly naked Tahitian skims
in an outrigger canoe. Though tales give voice to universal experiences like the pain and sorrow of lost love, and
the exultation and sense of renewal of found love, the
characters do not walk on air. They are all the more
powerful for their tangible humanity as they walk beside a
Navaho hogan, a Bushman's scherm, or a squire's estate.

When you consider time and place in a story, you
discover your assumptions, thoughts, feelings, and
sensations related to:

> climate
> geography
> topography
> population groups
> food
> clothing
> architecture
> options for work
> options for play
> threats to survival
> class distinctions of the culture
> the culture's definitions of
> > goodness
> > beauty

> strength
> health
> wealth

Stories live in and grow out of a landscape and its peoples.
The roots are tangible and potent; geography, history,
ethnicity, temporal and religious values—all of these
contribute to a culture and its manifestation in story.

Traveling to the locale of a given story can deepen
our experience of details in the story like nothing else
can. For example, I once stood next to a railroad track
that cut directly through a small town in Minnesota.
The power of the train, as it whizzed by, was exhilarating and magnificent. Its contrast in sheer size and
energy with the sluggish commuter trains with which I
was more familiar couldn't have been more startling.
Suddenly, Carl Sandburg's railroad rides woven throughout his *Rootabaga Stories* possessed dimensions of a raw
power and wild freedom previously unknown to me.
When the train rushed off across the flat horizon, I felt
its dynamism—vibrating the ground as compelling as a
waterfall—and heard its thrilling music.

RAPUNZEL: A CASE STUDY

Learning about time and place is not a substitute for
firsthand experience, but it is invaluable to the storyteller.

When William Irwin Thompson examines the role of
the herb rampion in the folktale of Rapunzel, he makes
the immutable quality of time and place in that story as
startling as the train in Minnesota. Rampion is the herb
Rapunzel's mother craves while she is pregnant with her.
Thompson writes:

> As one pulls gently on the plant, the roots pull up a
> more deeply buried artifact of a lost world. When I
> asked myself: "Why is this particular plant chosen for
> the story?" I was not prepared for all the delightful
> surprises that were hidden in the earth still clinging
> to the roots of this story.
>
> Rapunzel, or rampion, is *Campanula rapunculus;* it
> is a biennial herb that can be planted in the fall and
> harvested in the winter, and so it is very popular for
> use in winter salads. Both the roots and leaves are
> edible…But what is most interesting about this plant
> is that it is…endowed with the capacity to fertilize
> itself. A tall stem or column rises up and tries to
> attract insects to bring it the pollen from other plants,
> but if no pollination occurs, the column will split in
> two (the one becomes two again) and halves will
> curl like braids or coils on a maiden's head, and this
> will bring the female stagmatic tissue into contact
> with the male pollen on the exterior surface of the

stylar column. To help in the process of gathering the male pollen to itself, the column is endowed with "collecting hairs." So Rapunzel does indeed have a tower, does indeed send out a call for the male to come and pollinate her, and does indeed have "collecting hairs" that allow her to draw up the male into intimate contact with her reproductive organs...

I had no idea that the sexual life of the plant would itself recapitulate the sexual drama of the fairy tale.[1]

For forty-two pages Thompson explores other dimensions of this story that describe the landscape of a lost world, the cosmology of "Old Europe" from 6000 to 4000 B.C.:

When the male, patrilineal society of warriors lost all interest in and sensitivity for the ancient cosmology, the wise sorceress with her botanical and astrological knowledge became caricatured as an evil old witch with a foul-smelling cauldron of toads and weeds, but even in the society of warriors, the stories the nurse-maid would tell would keep the narrative structure intact as the material made its way from myth to legend to oral fairy tale and on into Romanticism and the high arts of a literate, industrial civilization.[2]

SETTINGS AND CULTURES:
KNOWING AND UNDERSTANDING

Stories usually address, in one way or another, what it means to be a human being—from the highest spiritual aspirations of a people to their most basic injunctions for daily living— within a specific cultural context. Stories resonate by juxtaposing universal experiences with unique ones. If the universality of a tale is its broth, then ethnic, religious, geographic, cultural, and historical details season the broth to flavor the stewpot of story.

Storytellers within a culture better understand which seasonings can be added freely and which require judicious measuring. Listeners within that same culture develop the palate to assess the tastiness of both the tale and the telling. Allowing for intracultural dissent, speaker and listener share basic understandings of that culture's definitions of satisfying storytelling. Whenever a storyteller comes from outside the culture of a given story, there is a tendency to emphasize the universal at the expense of cultural honesty and vigor. The people who created the recipe are all but forgotten. Metaphorically speaking, the tale can become so diluted as to become insubstantial; it can also be so inappropriately seasoned it becomes unrecognizable, unpalatable, or even putrid to those it once fed.[3]

One of the greatest powers of storytelling is to build bridges between cultures. Nonetheless, Melissa Heckler points out, you cannot build a span without footings on both shores. You have to take responsibility for *not* being part of a culture, as surely as you need to take responsibility for speaking from *within* your own cultural viewpoint. A student told me a Bahamian island has three signs at immigration: VISITORS, RESIDENTS, and BELONGERS. Fitting into any one of those classifications isn't problematic; rather, problems arise when people pretend to fit into a category that is not their own. Additionally, visitors must respect signs to avoid becoming trespassers.

The following questions guide your imagination; they do not address ethical questions of a storyteller's responsibilities when telling a story outside of her culture. These ethical questions are better confronted in other books and periodicals.[4] The questions in this book are offered as points of discovery. They might point up areas where additional research is required when cultural standards are unfamilar to you or where stereotypes have cut you off from a deeper understanding.

There is no single solution to the problems inherent in telling stories from outside of one's own culture. Telling stories requires intelligence and integrity. Research, insight, and ethical behavior are vital to the processes of storytelling. We need to examine a story; question our motives for telling it; in telling it, keep ourselves open to feedback; weigh the feedback that is offered; and return again to the story, our research, and our personal inventory. Vital questions are:

- Why do I want to tell this story?
- Do I need permission to tell this story?
- Has permission been granted?
- Do I know enough to tell this story responsibly?

The following three examples come from my own experience of telling stories distinctly outside my cultural and ethnic mix. The first example demonstrates how dramatically a story is shaped by feedback—the ongoing process of storytelling. In one way or another, telling outside your culture requires educated risks. Education is a process itself.

TAYZANNE: OUT OF HAITI

Since I began telling "Tayzanne," audiences comprised of both Haitians and non-Haitians have taught me a great deal more about the culture from which the story comes. In the late 1970s, I heard Binnie Tate, a storyteller in Los Angeles, tell the story. Years later, I read it

in Diane Wolkstein's anthology of Haitian stories,
The Magic Orange Tree.[5] The story, with its affecting song,
haunted me long after I heard it told. Reading the
commentaries included in Wolkstein's anthology, it
seemed appropriate to trust the extensive cultural
homework she had done in preparing the story for
readers and storytellers outside Haiti.

For those of us who face the responsibility of introducing a community of children to numerous cultures,
this is often the best we can do—find reliable sources.
The school librarian with twenty-seven programs each
week does not have the time or the luxury to research
every story he or she presents.

Stories from all over the world present interactions
between animals and human beings as a completely
natural occurrence. However, contemporary minds tend
to be overly literal, blinding listeners to the poetic truths
and richness in a story's metaphors and allegorical
connotations. Most storytellers tell stories in part because
they know in their bones what the writer Ursula LeGuin
asserted: realism may be the least effective way to talk
about the incredible realities of life.[6] Listeners may need
to be reminded of this—sometimes with subtle indirec-
tion, sometimes with boldness. Storytellers need to be
cognizant of the shifts required for auditoriums of kids
or conference ballrooms of adults to stay with this story

where a fish and a girl fall in love. An important aspect
of storytelling is reminding ourselves and listeners that
"truth" cannot be confined in a definition that includes
only demonstrable facts, for truth is more complex,
with intrinsic emotional and spiritual dimensions.

Most people tend to identify with the horror of the
struggle between Valina and her mother in the story
"Tayzanne." This mother spies on her daughter, judges
the love her daughter experiences as evil, enjoins her
son to trap Tayzanne, and spurs her husband to kill
him. Although these secretive, suspicious, and ulti-
mately brutal actions are disturbing, the plight of the
little brother most horrifies me, because he inadver-
tently advances the destructive actions.

He spies on Valina first just to learn where she
collects water, so he can do likewise. He wants to please
his mother, who has scolded him severely for bringing
water home each afternoon that is less clean than the
water his sister brings each morning. He returns home
and tells his mother, with some exuberance, the corrective actions he can take to get cleaner water for them all.
He answers her questions about what he has seen and
heard. This conversation precipitates all the destruction
that follows.

The mother further implicates him in his sister's
seeming death by having him sing Valina's song to call

Tayzanne. The mother's harsh mimicry of her daughter's voice has not fooled the fish, so she tells her son to sing, since his voice is sweet like his sister's. He obeys as a child must obey. Tayzanne answers the call and is killed by the father. Valina's overwhelming grief results in her tears softening the ground so that she sinks into the earth. Valina answers Tayzanne's call, for his voice is heard on the wind echoing the last line of the song she sang: *"Come to me!"*

The father sleeps through the concluding scenes of sorrow; the mother has her righteousness for consolation; the brother is without comfort. He has tried to save his sister by desperately pleading with his parents to help save Valina, and by this action we know he cared deeply about her. This is the horror of life—when harm comes from our limited attempts to do the right thing. In trying to please his mother and in obeying her, he saw his family rent apart on many levels.

Melinda Munger, a storyteller in Florida, told me she asked an elderly Haitian woman if it was true that in Haiti "Tayzanne" is a beloved and popular story. The woman affirmed it was true. She also told her that Valina and Tayzanne are the parents of all the mermaids in the world. What an astonishing reversal: the subtext, recognized within the Haitian community, shifts the entire meaning of the story. Instead of the story being about the cruel

destruction of a family and the loss of two lives, it is
understood to highlight the redemptive and fertile
power of love!

This information about the story "Tayzanne" exem-
plifies how profoundly storytelling is a process for teller
and listeners alike. I came to the story as many do. On
hearing it, I was struck by its power, then searched for a
printed source, learned the printed version, and discovered over the years details both large and small that
continue to shape the telling.

A SCANDINAVIAN PILGRIMAGE

I came to Norwegian folktales by a completely
different route. As an undergraduate at St. Olaf College
in Minnesota, I discovered an affinity with Scandinavian
decorative arts that left me eager to travel there. I also
discovered the existential philosophy of Søren Kierkegaard.
His philosophy addresses precisely the pain of Valina's
brother in "Tayzanne": pain captured visually in Edvard
Munch's painting *The Scream*. Although the psychic pain
depicted by Munch and of which Kierkegaard wrote is
universal, it is difficult to imagine them producing such
work from the French Riviera. Their work is inextricably
woven from the threads of a harsher natural environment
and the industrialization of modern cultures.

While completing course work in a doctoral program at the University of Southern California, I made a modern-day pilgrimage to Ojai, California, to visit the great storyteller Frances Clarke Sayers. Mrs. Sayers had written a passage in *Summoned by Books* that had been and remains a touchstone for me as a storyteller:

> The future contribution of storytelling may well surpass all that has gone before. In an age when all the world's not a stage, but a screen, a picture, a delineation of the obvious object and the obvious symbol for emotion; in an age when the imagination is dulled and stunted by a surfeit of pictures in magazines, textbooks, billboards, buses and newspapers—in such an age the art of the storyteller remains, giving his listeners the space, the time, and the words with which to build in their imaginations the...shapes and sounds none knows or hears save each mind for itself.[7]

At the conclusion of my visit, Mrs. Sayers told me I *must* do my dissertation on Gudrun Thorne-Thomsen. I did not know the name, or even if it was the name of a man or woman. Mrs. Sayers, with her firm grasp on my shoulders and direct stare into my eyes, was not about to accept evasion. I assured her I would follow through on her suggestion. The *next day*, when I entered my office at USC, the recordings of Gudrun Thorne-Thomsen stared up from my desk. In clearing out her office, my academic advisor had found some old recordings made by the Library of Congress in the 1940s. Since the recordings featured a storyteller, she thought I might want to listen to them. It seemed like what Carl Sandburg called "a sign and a signal."[8] I decided to do my dissertation on this Norwegian woman who came to America and so astounded listeners that she came to the attention of one of the grand institutions in America.

No universities in the Los Angeles area taught Norwegian, but amazingly my local adult school in Manhattan Beach offered beginning, intermediate, and advanced Norwegian. I took all three courses as well as private tutoring, over the next two years. In the autumn of 1982, I traveled to Norway to study at the University of Bergen. My work compared English versions of Norwegian folktales as translated by Sir George Dassant, Sigrid Unset, and Gudrun Thorne-Thomsen with the Norwegian versions set down by the folklorists Asbjorsen and Moe, who collected stories in Norway as the Brothers Grimm did in Germany.

Rather close study of these particular folktales does not allow me to tell them with the kind of authority and intimacy a Norwegian storyteller brings. Though both of us could speak with fluency and immediacy, these qualities would be anchored in different aspects of the story. Nuances of meaning experienced over a lifetime, particulars of landscape and culture, as well as colloquial idioms and puns would escape my notice. When I returned to America I realized with startling clarity that in Norway I had had no sense of the ironic. If the ironical was lost to me, imagine how much else I missed that is embedded in the tales! An educated visitor is still a visitor.

THE NARRATOR AS CULTURAL PRISM

Not often, but sometimes, it is possible to reside in stories from other cultures because of the profound similarity of human experiences. My childhood was inalterably shaped by my father's zealous desire for his children to be *American*—not Buczkowski, but Birch. Assimilation, necessary for survival in the first three decades of the twentieth century, became an identity and source of pride. I jokingly say we never cooked cabbage at home, so fully did my father deny his Polish heritage. Like many sons of immigrants, he rejected all things "foreign"; he embraced American traditions and ideals.

In *The Dream Book: An Anthology of Writings by Italian American Women*, edited by Helen Barolini, I found a home.[9] As all superb anthologies do, it led me back to the works of the featured writers. In Dorothy Bryant's novel, *Miss Giardino,* the personal fears and doubts that I thought isolated me were placed in a broader cultural context of immigration that can cut across ethnic lines.[10] The details, polenta instead of pierogies, and the language, Italian not Polish, were different. The emotional depths were familiar: fierce love; feelings of being an outsider reinforced by the quick identification of the ethnicity of all strangers; and the (unacknowledged) tendency in my parents to measure "us" against "them"—"them" being all other identifiable immigrant groups. An inexplicable sense of *not* being good enough was reinforced by the protests "We're as good as..." Actions were interpreted through the filter of "proving" our worth. Much of my life story was there on the page.

Whether I am telling "Tayzanne," "The Three Billy Goats Gruff," an excerpt from *The Dream Book,* or *Miss Giardino,* a thread binds the stories together. The thread is a Scots-Irish/Welsh/Polish woman born in Pittsburgh, Pennsylvania, who lives within several familial, geographic, and cultural groups in the United States at the turn of the twenty-first century. I am the common denominator in all the stories I tell. I am always the person speaking; like Popeye, "I yam what I yam." Pretending to be Italian, Norwegian, or Haitian would be inherently fraudulent. Accepting my outsideness allows me to speak with my own kind of strength and conviction. When I tell these stories, they are refracted through the prism of my life.

FULL DISCLOSURE: THE STORYTELLER'S TASK

Can the prism of our lives distort the stories we tell? Yes. So we need to follow a vigilant and vigorous course as we filter stories through our intelligence and integrity. Should we never tell stories outside our culture? Every storyteller who moves beyond personal stories eventually faces this dilemma.

My colleague Melissa Heckler grappled with this issue in her work in Ju/'hoan culture. She believes that when someone from within a culture speaks to others of the same culture, intracultural dialogues flourish. When a storyteller tells stories from another culture, it can promote crosscultural dialogues. However, if a storyteller pretends to be part of a culture he or she is not related to, the misrepresentation stifles the possibility of real dialogue. To an audience unfamiliar with the story's culture, the best that can be achieved is a performance *tour de force*. The spotlight stays on the storyteller, leaving both the complexity and truths of the culture—

as well as the audience—literally in the dark. It is the essence of storytelling as disingenuous entertainment. Make no mistake, this is neither an indictment of storytelling as entertainment nor of a storyteller's skillful achievements. It is an indictment of the mendacious qualities when boldness lacks intelligence and integrity.

When a story is deliberately fractured—removed from its original setting—it can still be quite genuine, because it declares its intentional distortions. Ed Stivender's outrageous retelling of "Cinderella" moves a courtly tale from France to the streets of Rocky Balboa's Philadelphia. "Yo, Cindy!" he calls, and the audience roars appreciatively. Cinderella dons a gold lamé jumpsuit. Tennis shoes replace the glass slippers. Years ago he said they were Adidas, though one of Cindy's sisters was hoping for Reeboks; now he might say Nikes.[11] His dazzling invention in the details of time and place reverberates throughout the tale, increasing the dramatic tension through irony and surprise. For the purpose of the example here, he in essence "pretends" nothing. There is no fraud, deceit, or misrepresentation as he ebulliently claims all creative distortion and invention.

In actuality, fracturing a story can be much more than a delight. It also provides one of the surest ways to identify the details of time and place that permeate a story. Characters live on a continent within some kind of country, region, or area where some kind of home or personal place exists. They live in a distinct age if not identifiable century, decade, year, month, or day. They live within, or in opposition to, regional cultures, several subcultures, and a designated family unit of some kind.

As a storyteller, the most important underlying issues to understand are:

- How does setting function in your story?
- What indicators of era and locale would appear in a mural of the story?
- What about this time and place binds the characters together?
- What is important historically about the time and place of your story?
- What about this time and place makes you want to return to it repeatedly?

The answers to these questions are the ones most vital to the process of grounding the story in a setting. The prompts on pages 93-108 are offered to lead to a more concrete understanding of these most fundamental issues.

If you have trouble with these prompts, set aside times over several weeks to orient yourself with senses other than your eyes. Periodically close your eyes to

focus on physical sensations and sounds around you in
a variety of settings. Listen as people work and play,
both indoors and outside. Sound can be thought of as
music. What music is in your tale? If you were making
an audiocassette of sounds to play under your story,
what would you include? Make yourself more aware of
fleeting scents and robust odors; notice your response to
textures and colors; savor the foods you eat. You cannot
bring an awareness to stories that is not part of your
awareness in life. Remember: the goal is to make the
story real and therefore more compelling to you so that
it will be held in all of your senses and not merely as
marks on a page.

If you continue to have difficulty identifying how
important the setting is in the story, retell the story,
changing the era and then the locale. Whatever alterations appear in the retelling indicate time and place in
the original story. Look at the story and consider what
remains when you remove all explicit and implicit
details of locale and era. You won't see much beyond
the bones of the sequence of the plot and stick figures
for characters.

SETTING PROMPTS

Go through the story to identify *explicit* indicators of time and place in your story.

At the beginning of a story, as best you can tell, what era, age, century, or year is it?

What is the season?

What time of day is it?

What is the climate?

What do you notice about the weather:

What is the temperature?

What physical sensations result from the weather?

Are there any sounds associated with it?

Can you smell anything?

Does the weather arouse any feelings in you?

Identify any effects weather and climate might have on the storyline and the characters.

Does the continent, country, or region for most of the action of the story change?

Identify differences in the terrains in which the characters move.

Describe the terrain of the main area in the story.

What is the ground like?

What color is it?

What is its texture?

When you pick up the dirt in your hands, what do you notice about how it feels?

How does it smell?

How much of the bare dirt can you see?

What limits your range of vision?

If you look out and turn all around, what are the land's distinguishing characteristics?

What indicators demonstrate wild or civilized aspects of the landscape?

What indicators demonstrate the care or carelessness of human presence?

How productive is the land?

Could it be more productive?

What is growing?

In this landscape, what kind of work is possible or required?

What kind of play fits into the setting?

If you look from the ground up to the sky, does the sky seem near or far?

Is the sky illuminated in any way?

Is there any movement in the sky?

How broad is your view of the sky?

What, if anything, constricts your view?

What's the farthest you can see?

Change your point of view. If you are aware of height, imagine being much lower; if you are very low, place yourself higher.

Now describe the setting from a new vantage point:

What do you see when you turn around?

Has the temperature changed?

Can you hear something you didn't hear before?

Are there any new scents?

When you extend your hands, can you touch anything?

Can you touch anything that was out of reach before?

What kinds of animals live here?

Wild?

Domesticated?

Pets?

How do they feature in the story?

List any subtle or obvious threats to survival.

If a character were going to move within this landscape to a place where they would feel more safe, where would that be?

Why would it seem more safe there?

Which characters would feel safe in this place?

Summarize the effects natural physical features have on events and people in the story.

Move toward man-made shelters or buildings. What can you tell about this era or this age from the architecture?

Are there many buildings, or just a few?

What is the style of architecture?

What building materials are used?

Color

Texture

Design elements

Do the buildings blend in with the landscape or do they seem forced upon it?

Is the placement of the buildings useful?

How harmonious are the structures?

Summarize what effect the placement of buildings has on events and people in the story.

Energies created by environments influence the way we feel in them. At its best, the word "home" conjures up images of belonging, affection, warmth, and security: refuge from the elements and emotional protection with intimate ties to family and community. When a character enters his or her home, or an important building in the story, what is noticeable about the transition from outside to inside?

What is the primary purpose of this building?

How simple or complex is the layout of the building?

What seems to be valued here?

Is there a change in temperature?

>Humidity?

>Light?

What noises can be heard?

What texture does the silence have?

What does the air smell like?

Enter a room. How is it separated from the rest of the structure?

>What is the first impression?

>How cluttered or spare is the room?

How colorful is it?

Is the room warm and welcoming, or off-putting in some way?

What seems to be valued in the room?

How important are artifacts of status, social position, and material wealth?

What in this room connects its occupants to the natural environment?

Has the light changed?

What can be heard?

Is there a new scent?

Has the temperature changed?

Describe the furnishings.

Consider the level of comfort offered, in terms of size, proportion, color, texture.

Are the furnishings artificially contrived or natural for local conditions?

Is anything on the walls?

How is the room heated?

How is the room ventilated?

How fresh does the air feel?

What are the primary and secondary sources of light?

What reaction do the characters have to the dimness or brightness of the light?

Do the floors enhance the comfort of the room?

If there are coverings on the floor, what are they made of?

Where is food prepared?

How is it prepared?

What is being cooked?

How is food served?

How pleasant is the whole experience of cooking, serving, and eating a meal in this setting?

From walking around—both outside and within a dwelling—what can you surmise about the economics of the area?

What indicators of wealth and poverty are apparent outside and in?

What, if any, class distinctions are apparent?

How much time literally elapses during the story?

Metaphorically, how much time, in terms of growth and change, passes?

Language in a story indicates details of time and place. To become aware of this, retell the story through any stereotypical character, like a California "Valley Girl," and you'll hear where words or speech patterns collide.

What indicators of time and place are noticeable in the words and style of narrative sections?

What indicators are noticeable in the characters' speech?

Overall, how formal/colloquial is the language used?

What group distinctions are reinforced in the way characters speak to one another?

What can you surmise about secular and religious values of this time and place?

During the entire process, have your assessments of the fundamental values changed?

How would these qualities be defined and prioritized:

Family

Friendship

Love

Affection

Strength

Goodness

Generosity

Humor

Community

Children

Old People

Education

Wisdom

Play

Beauty

Art

Commerce

Wealth

Government

Faith

Finally, returning to the questions posed on page 90:

How does setting function in your story?

What indicators of era and locale would appear in a mural of the story?

What about this time and place binds the characters together?

What is important historically about the time and place of your story?

What about this time and place makes you want to return to it repeatedly?

AFTER THE QUESTIONS

Whew! I hope you believed me when I said that I do not have answers to all these questions and that not all the questions would be helpful. The questions were just prompts; trust *your* process. I hope they have provided you a cluster of images that will enhance the imaginative intensity of the pictures in your mind.

In America, the dominant modern mall culture loves quick reads and quick courses to solve problems, quickly! "Been there, done that"—the hip approach to life. This book is the antithesis of that common refrain. It asks you to wander around and within a story, not advance briskly through it. Like the great book *The Way of the Storyteller*, these questions are a call to go questing, to provide an antidote to:

a deadly and vicious cycle of picking a story out of some collection, learning it by rote, telling it, and going back to the collection again. It is a dreadful thing to think about—a kind of additional limbo to

Dante's inferno. It means that the true significance of storytelling is lost, or never discovered. It means there is never a knowing of the untold joy of the artist in taking substance, giving it form and color, blowing the breath of life into it, and then watching it take on life for others.[1]

When we get up to tell stories, all too often we edit out our naturally expressive impulses. Playing with character and setting provides us with a way to speak with attitudes and conviction about the people and places in a story. It helps us avoid the more mechanical posturing in recitation, the studied techniques of poor acting, while moving us more easily into natural and spirited conversational styles. When most people are engaged in spirited conversations, they have an attitude about what they are saying and they use their voices, faces, and bodies naturally in expressive and compelling ways without effort or self-consciousness. Knowing more than is on the page helps me find the attitudes to do the same when telling stories found in print.

Please note: after consideration of these questions and/or ruminations about the larger story imagined around the one given, *it is time to return to the text*. The appropriateness of attitudes is measured there. We can make corrections to follow the author's lead, or decide

on what basis we are diverging from the images suggested by the text. Changes will occur; yet it is vital to
seriously question reasons for altering the thrust, tone,
or symmetry of a story.

For nearly half my storytelling career, I stopped
telling *Rootabaga Stories* because both the foundation
and the publisher wanted monies beyond my means for
introducing these tales to new generations of children.
When I did, however, I consciously chose not to refer to
the main characters in "The White Horse Girl and The
Blue Wind Boy" as *two darlings*.[2] Since I was near their
age, involved in similar processes of leaving home and
searching for a place in the world, my delivery lacked
authority. Now I easily look back on their youthful-
ness—and mine—with all the nostalgia and tenderness
the petname *darlings* implies. I'm finally old enough to
tell the story.

Using the imagination to explore story moves text off
a page. From examining details, large discoveries emerge.
Story is held viscerally with associative memories of
sensation, and not by the tiny section of our brains that is
linear and structures rote memorization. As storytellers
we move beyond frozen moments of performance
techniques to the more fluid, mutable, and innumerable responses of emotional honesty *in support of the
text*. The substance and resonance of the story remain,

but listeners are also afforded a storyteller who presents a true measure of himself in concert with a story.

Questions like these move a story from the absolute uniformity of the print tradition to the more fluid oral tradition. Subsequent printings of a story are exactly the same. In the oral tradition, subsequent tellings of a story are not exactly the same. In speaking of those who learn music from a recording, David Thomsen said: It "creates a uniformity unknown to their grandparents who never sang the same song in the same way twice."[3] Improvisation plays a vital role in storytelling, it includes the beauty of tradition while growing out of experience, originality, and the generative power of an audience. The oral tradition celebrates an inherent fluidity, creativity, and natural development in the life of a story. When authors *tell* stories they've penned, their language becomes more fluid as they adapt their material in response to the people before them. Sandburg did it as he traveled across America; Jane Yolen does it today.

I do not memorize stories, and yet I know them absolutely. I've heard that someone asked musician Artur Rubinstein how he memorized all those black marks on a page. His response is the same as the storyteller's; the goal is not to memorize the strokes on a page, as notes or words, but to *know where the tune is*

going. In a similar vein, Ruth Sawyer wrote: "Sorry indeed
are the performance and the performer when all that is
given is what a public stenographer could note down on
paper…when all that is given in the telling is no more
than what may lie already on the printed page."[4]

Learn the shape of the story, where its tune is going.
Take cues from the text, research all you can. Imagine all
you need to know about the faces and hearts of the
characters, the stresses and conflicts they encounter, and
the possibilities for victory they can achieve. *And tell that.*
Move beyond stock castle, beyond stereotyped wood-
cutters and warriors, beyond typical journeys. Localize,
particularize, specify, clarify—and you'll know the story
beyond all question of memorizing and forgetting.

Storytelling requires a depth of feeling, integrity,
intelligence, and imagination. A little boldness helps
also. So bring the best you have to the fore, then sin
boldly, and do tell! For as Emily Dickinson wrote:

> A word is dead
> When it is said,
> Some say.
>
> I say it just
> Begins to live
> That day.[5]

NOTES

Introduction

1. Jane Yolen, *Touch Magic: Fantasy, Faerie and Folklore in the Literature of Childhood* (New York: Philomel, 1981), 9.

2. Joseph Sobol, *The Storyteller's Journey: An American Revival* (Urbana: University of Illinois Press, 1999).

3. Eleanor Farjeon, "Elsie Piddock Skips In Her Sleep" in *Martin Pippin in the Daisy Field* (New York: Frederich A. Stokes, 1937), 64–90.

4. Richard Kennedy, "Come Again in the Spring" in *Richard Kennedy: Collected Stories* (New York: Harper & Row, 1987), 12.

5. Carl Sandburg, "The Huckabuck Family and How They Raised Pop Corn in Nebraska and Quit and Came Back" in *Rootabaga Stories* (New York: Harcourt, Brace & World, 1922), 2:174.

6. Joseph Jacobs, "Mr. Fox" in *English Fairy Tale* (New York: Dover, 1967), 148–151.

7. Carl Sandburg, "Poetry Considered," *Atlantic Monthly*, March 1923.

8. Melissa Heckler, "Two Traditions" in *Who Says? Essays on Pivotal Issues in Contemporary Storytelling*, ed. Carol L. Birch and Melissa Heckler (Little Rock: August House, 1996), 23.

9. Arthur Machen, *The Hill of Dreams* (London: Richards Press, 1907).

10. Ruth Sawyer, *The Way of the Storyteller* (New York: Viking Press, 1942).

11. Cynthia Helms, "Storytelling, Gender and Language in Folk/Fairy Tales," *Women and Language* 10, no. 2.

12. Geoffrey Chaucer, "The Wife of Bath's Tale" in *The Canterbury Tales* (New York: Bantam Books, 1964).

13. Selina Hastings, *Sir Gawain and the Loathly Lady* (New York: Lothrop, Lee and Shepard Books, 1985).

14. Heather Forest, "The Tale of Dame Ragnel" in *More Best Loved Stories Told at the National Storytelling Festival* (Jonesborough, TN: The National Storytelling Presss, 1992), 169. Also on audio-cassette: *The Eye of Beholder* (Cambridge: Yellow Moon Press, 1990).

15. Marina Warner, review of *Sacred Pleasure: Sex, Myth, and the Politics of the Body* by Riane Eisler, *New York Times Book Review,* 18 June 1995.

16. For additional reading on this model, see my essay "Who Says? The Storyteller as Narrator" in *Who Says? Essays on Pivotal Issues in Contemporary Storytelling,* ed. Carol L. Birch and Melissa Heckler (Little Rock: August House, 1996), 106–128.

Working with Texts

1. Wanda Gag, *Millions of Cats* (New York: Coward-McCann, 1928).

2. Truman Capote, *The Thanksgiving Visitor* (New York: Random House, 1967).

3. Laurence Housman, "The Wooing of the Maze" in *The Rat Catcher's Daughter: A Collection of Stories by Laurence Housman,* ed. Ellin Greene (New York: Atheneum, 1974), 57.

4. Kathy Bates, interview by James Lipton, *Inside the Actors Studio,* Bravo television network, 1999.

Character

1. Cynthia De Felice, *Lostman's River* (New York: Maxwell Macmillan, 1994), 7.

2. Mordacai Gerstein, *The Shadow of a Flying Bird* (New York: Hyperion Books, 1994).

3. Helen Eustis, *Death and the Red-Headed Woman* (San Diego: Green Tiger Press, 1983).

4. Ray Bradbury, *The Halloween Tree* (New York: Knopf, 1972), 9–10.

5. Ibid, 10–11.

6. ———, introduction to *Dandelion Wine* (New York: Bantam Books, 1975), ix.

Setting

1. William Irwin Thompson, "Rapunzel: Cosmology Lost" in *Imaginary Landscape: Making Worlds of Myth and Science* (New York: St. Martin's Press, 1989), 31–34.

2. Ibid, 33–34.

3. Carol Birch, "Storytelling: Practice and Movement" in *Teaching Oral Traditons,* ed. John Miles Foley (New York: Modern Language Association, 1998), 314.

4. For a fuller discussion of issues and ethics when telling stories outside your own cultural traditions see: Susan Klein, "Storytelling Ethics" in *Storytelling World* 15 (winter/spring 1999) and essays by Toelken, Schram, Bruchac, Stone, and Guenther in *Who Says? Essays on Pivotal Issues in Contemporary Storytelling,* ed. Carol L. Birch and Melissa Heckler (Little Rock: August House, 1996).

5. Diane Wolkstein, "Tayzanne" in *The Magic Orange Tree and Other Haitian Folktales* (New York: Schocken, 1980), 60–63.

6. Ursula LeGuin, *The Language of the Night* (New York: G.P. Putnam's, 1979), 53.

7. Frances Clarke Sayers, *Summoned by Books* (New York: Viking Press, 1965), 97.

8. Carl Sandburg, "The Huckabuck Family and How They Raised Pop Corn in Nebraska and Quit and Came Back" in *Rootabaga Stories* (New York: Harcourt, Brace & World, 1922), 2:175.

9. Helen Barolini, ed., *The Dream Book: An Anthology of Writings by Italian American Women* (New York: Schocken Books, 1985).

10. Dorothy Bryant, *Miss Giardino* (Berkeley: Ata Books, 1978).

11. Ed Stivender, "Cinderella" on *Tales of Humor and Wit*, (Jonesborough, TN: National Storytelling Press, 1991).

Conclusion

1. Ruth Sawyer, *The Way of the Storyteller* (New York: Viking Press, 1942), 36.

2. Carl Sandburg, "The White Horse Girl and the Blue Wind Boy" in *Rootabaga Stories* (New York: Harcourt, Brace & World, 1922), 1:163.

3. David Thomsen, *The People of the Sea* (London: Paladin, 1965), 12.

4. Sawyer, *The Way of the Storyteller*, p. 32.

5. *Emily Dickenson: Poetry for Young People*, ed. Frances Schoonmaker (New York: Sterling Publishing, 1994).

BIBLIOGRAPHY

Since this book presents only one approach on "how to" tell stories, I wanted to include books with other approaches to the art of storytelling. Books by storytellers demonstrate their models for working with stories. Books with an ethnographic orientation offer different models by focusing on the contextual support for storytelling in a variety of communities. A few of the books listed here fundamentally shaped my storytelling; others provide years of rumination, like chewing gum for the mind; some fill an increasingly long reading wish list.

Many storytellers suggested favorite titles for this bibliography, and I am grateful for their support: Janice Del Negro, Heather Forest, Marni Gillard, Martha Hamilton, Bill Harley, David Holt, Priscilla Howe, Tim Jennings, Susan Klein, Margaret Read MacDonald, Barbara McBride-Smith, Rafe Martin, Lee-Ellen Marvin, Eric Miller, Jay O'Callahan, J.G. Pinkerton, Judy Sima, Laura Simms, Joseph Sobol, Corinne Stavish, Kay Stone, Ruth Stotter, and Mitch Weiss.

Azadovskii, Mark. *A Siberian Tale Teller.* Translated by James R. Dow. Austin: University of Texas Press, 1974.

Braden, Waldo Warder. *The Oral Tradition in the South.* Baton Rouge: Louisiana State University Press, 1983.

Bailey, Carolyn Sherwin. *For the Story Teller: Story Telling and Stories to Tell.* Springfield, MA: Milton Bradley Co, 1925.

Barton, Bob. *Tell Me Another: Storytelling and Reading Aloud at Home and in the Community.* Portsmouth, NH: Heinemann, 1986.

———— and David Booth. *Stories in the Classroom: Storytelling, Reading Aloud and Roleplaying with Children.* Portsmouth, NH: Heinemann, 1990.

Bauer, Caroline Feller. *Caroline Feller Bauer's New Handbook for Storytellers: With Stories, Poems, Magic and More.* Chicago: American Library Association, 1993.

Bauman, Richard. *Folklore, Cultural Performances and Popular Entertainments.* New York: Oxford University Press, 1992.

————. *Story, Performance, and Event.* Cambridge: Cambridge University Press, 1986.

Birch, Carol, and Melissa Heckler, ed. *Who Says? Essays on Pivotal Issues in Contemporary Storytelling.* Little Rock: August House, 1996.

Breneman, Lucille, and Bren Breneman. *Once Upon a Time: A Storytelling Handbook.* Chicago: Nelson-Hall, 1983.

Briggs, Charles L. *Competence in Performance: The Creativity of Tradition in Mexicano Verbal Art.* Philadelphia: University of Pennsylvania Press, 1988.

Bruchac, Joseph. *Tell Me a Tale: A Book about Storytelling.* San Diego: Harcourt Brace, 1997.

Bryant, Sara Cone. *How To Tell Stories to Children.* Detroit: Gale, 1973.

Cabral, Len, and Mia Manduca. *Len Cabral's Storytelling Book.* New York: Neal-Schuman Publishers, 1997.

Cassady, Marsh. *The Art of Storytelling: Creative Ideas for Preparation and Performance.* Colorado Springs: Meriwether Publications, 1994.

————. *Storytelling Step by Step.* San Jose, CA: Resource Publications, 1990.

Cather, Katherine Dunlap. *Educating by Storytelling*. New York: World Book, 1920.

Chambers, Dewey W. *The Oral Tradition: Storytelling and Creative Drama*. Dubuque, IA: W. C. Brown, 1977.

Chalmers, Aidan. "Storytelling and Reading Aloud." In *Introducing Books to Children*. London: Heinemann, 1973.

Colum, Padraic. *Story Telling New and Old*. New York: Macmillan, 1961.

Colwell, Eileen H. *A Second Storyteller's Choice: A Selection of Stories with Notes on How To Tell Them*. New York: H. Z. Walck, 1965.

————. *Storytelling*. London: Bodley Head, 1980.

Cook, Elizabeth. *The Ordinary and the Fabulous: An Introduction to Myths, Legends, and Fairy Tales for Teachers and Storytellers*. London: Cambridge University Press, 1969.

Cooper, Pamela J., and Rives Collins. *Look What Happened to Frog: Storytelling in Education*. Scottsdale, AZ: Gorsuch Scarisbrick, 1992.

Crowley, Daniel J. *I Could Talk Old-Story Good: Creativity in Bahamian Folklore*. Berkeley: University of California Press, 1966.

Cullum, Carolyn N. *The Storytime Sourcebook: A Compendium of Ideas and Resources for Storytellers*. New York: Neal-Schuman, 1990.

Cunningham, Keith. *American-Indians' Kitchen-Table Stories: Contemporary Conversations with Cherokee, Sioux, Hopi, Osage, Navajo, Zuni, and Members of Other Nations*. Little Rock: August House, 1992.

Dailey, Sheila. *Putting the World in a Nutshell: The Art of the Formula Tale*. Bronx, NY: H.W. Wilson, 1994.

————. *Tales as Tools: The Power of Storytelling in the Classroom*. Jonesborough, TN: National Storytelling Press, 1996.

Davis, Donald. *Telling Your Own Stories: For Family and Classroom Storytelling, Public Speaking, and Personal Journaling*. Little Rock: August House, 1993.

Davis, Gerald L. *I Got the Word in Me and I Can Sing It, You Know: A Study of the Performed African-American Sermon*. Philadelphia: University of Pennsylvania Press, 1985.

Degh, Linda. *Folktales and Society: Storytelling in a Hungarian Peasant Community*. Bloomington: Indiana University Press, 1969.

De Vos, Gail. *Storytelling for Young Adults: Techniques and Treasury.* Englewood, CO: Libraries Unlimited, 1991.

————. *Tales, Rumors, and Gossip: Exploring Contemporary Folk Literature in Grades 7–12.* Englewood, CO: Libraries Unlimited, 1996.

De Wit, Dorothy. *Children's Faces Looking Up: Program Building for the Storyteller.* Chicago: American Library Association, 1979.

Dorson, Richard. *Bloodstoppers and Bearwalkers: Folktales of Canadians, Lumberjacks and Indians.* Cambridge: Harvard University Press, 1952.

Farrell, Catherine. *Storytelling: A Guide for Teachers.* New York: Scholastic, 1991.

Fine, Elizabeth. *The Folklore Text: From Performance to Print.* Bloomington: Indiana University Press, 1984.

Fitzgerald, Burdette S. *World Tales for Creative Dramatics and Storytelling.* Englewood Cliffs, NJ: Prentice-Hall, 1962.

Foley, John Miles, ed. *Oral Tradition in Literature: Interpretation in Context.* Columbia: University of Missouri Press, 1986.

————. *Teaching Oral Traditions.* New York: The Modern Language Association, 1998.

Glassie, Henry. *Irish Folktales.* New York: Pantheon, 1997.

————. *Passing the Time in Ballymenone: Culture and History in an Ulster Community.* Philadelphia: University of Pennsylvania Press, 1977.

Gillard, Marni. *Storyteller, Storyteacher: Discovering the Power of Storytelling for Teaching and Living.* York, ME: Stenhouse, 1996.

Goldberg, Natalie. *Writing Down the Bones.* Boston: Shambhala Publications, 1986.

Greene, Ellin. *Storytelling: Art and Technique.* 3rd ed. New Providence, NJ: Reed Reference Publishing, 1996.

Hamilton, Martha and Mitch Weiss. *Children Tell Stories: A Teaching Guide.* Katonah, NY: Richard C. Owen Publishers, 1990.

————. *Stories in My Pocket: Tales Kids Can Tell.* Golden, CO: Fulcrum, 1996.

Hayes, Joe. *Here Comes the Storyteller.* El Paso, TX: Cinco Puntos Press, 1996.

Heath, Shirley Brice. *Ways with Words: Language, Life, and Work in Communities and Classrooms.* Cambridge: Cambridge University Press, 1983.

Helms, Cynthia. "Storytelling, Gender and Language in Folk/Fairy Tales." *Women and Language* 10, no. 2.

Herman, Gail N. *Storytelling: A Triad in the Arts.* Mansfield Center, CT: Creative Learning Press, 1986.

Horn Book Magazine. Storytelling issue: June 1983.

Hurston, Zora Neale. *Mules and Men.* 1935. Reprint, New York: Negro University Press, 1969.

Keen, Sam, and Anne Valley-Fox. *Your Mythic Journey: Finding Meaning in Your Life Through Writing and Storytelling.* Los Angeles: Jeremy P. Tarcher, 1989.

Klein, Susan. *And Now, Would You Please Welcome...: A Guide for Emceeing Storytelling Events.* Oak Bluffs, MA: Ruby Window Productions, 1993.

————. "Storytelling Ethics." *Storytelling World* no. 15 (winter/spring 1999).

Lane, Marcia. *Picturing the Rose: A Way of Looking at Fairy Tales.* Bronx, NY: H.W. Wilson, 1994.

Lipke, Barbara. *Figures, Facts and Fables: Telling Tales in Science and Math.* Portsmouth, NH: Heinemann, 1996.

Lipman, Doug. *The Storytelling Coach: How to Listen, Praise, and Bring Out People's Best.* Little Rock: August House, 1995.

Livo, Norma J., and Sandra A. Rietz. *Storytelling: Process and Practice.* Littleton, CO: Libraries Unlimited, 1986.

Lord, Albert B. *The Singer of Tales.* Cambridge: Harvard University Press, 1960.

MacDonald, Margaret Read. *The Parent's Guide to Storytelling.* New York: HarperCollins, 1995.

————. *Scipio Storytelling: Talk in a Southern Indiana Community.* Lanham, NY: University Press of America, 1996.

————. *Storyteller's Sourcebook: A Subject, Title, and Motif Index to Folklore Collections for Children.* Detroit, MI: Neal-Schuman Publishers, 1982.

————. *The Storyteller's Start-Up Book: Finding, Learning, Performing, and Using Folktales.* Little Rock: August House, 1993.

————. *Traditional Storytelling Today: An International Sourcebook.* Chicago: Fitzroy Dearborn Publishers, 1999.

Maguire, Jack. *Creative Storytelling: Choosing, Inventing and Sharing Tales for Children.* Cambridge: Yellow Moon Press, 1985.

————. *The Power of Personal Storytelling: Spinning Tales to Connect with Others.* New York: J.P. Tarcher/Putnam, 1998.

Martin, Calvin Luther. *The Way of the Human Being.* New Haven, CT: Yale University Press, 1999.

Mathia, Elizabeth, and Richard Raspa. *Italian Folktales in America: The Verbal Art of Immigrant Women.* Detroit: Wayne State University Press, 1988.

McKenna, Megan, and Tony Cowan. *Keepers of the Story: Oral Traditions in Religion.* Maryknoll, NY: Orbis Books, 1997.

Mellon, Nancy. *Storytelling and the Art of Imagination.* Rockport, MA: Element, 1992.

Miller, Teresa. *Joining-In: An Anthology of Audience Participation Stories and How To Tell Them.* Cambridge: Yellow Moon Press, 1988.

Mills, Margaret. *Rhetorics and Politics in Afghan Traditional Storytelling.* Philadelphia: University of Pennsylvania Press, 1991.

Mooney, Bill, and David Holt. *The Storyteller's Guide: Storytellers Share Advice for the Classroom, Boardroom, Showroom, Podium, Pulpit, and Center Stage.* Little Rock: August House, 1996.

Moore, Robin. *Awakening the Hidden Storyteller: How to Build a Storytelling Tradition in Your Family.* Berkeley, CA: Shambhala, 1991; reprinted as *Creating a Family Storytelling Tradition*, Little Rock: August House, 1999.

Narayan, Kirin. *Mondays On the Dark Night of the Moon: Himalayan Foothill Folktales.* New York: Oxford University Press, 1997.

————. *Storytellers, Saints, and Scoundrels: Folk Narrative in Hindu Religious Teaching.* Philadelphia: University of Pennsylvania Press, 1989.

Pellowski, Anne. *The Family Storytelling Handbook: How to Use Stories, Anecdotes, Rhymes, Handkerchiefs, Paper and Other Objects to Enrich*

Your Family Traditions. New York: Collier Macmillan, 1987.

————. *The Story Vine: A Source Book of Unusual and Easy-To-Tell Stories from Around the World.* New York: Collier/Aladdin, 1984.

————. *The Storytelling Handbook: A Young People's Collection of Unusual Tales and Helpful Hints on How To Tell Them.* New York: Simon & Schuster, 1995.

————. *The World of Storytelling.* New York: Bowker, 1977.

Price, Richard, and Sally Price. *Two Evenings in Saramaka.* Chicago: University of Chicago Press, 1991.

Rodari, Gianni. *The Grammar of Fantasy: An Introduction to the Art of Inventing Stories.* Translated by Jack Zipes. New York: Teachers and Writers Collaborative, 1996.

Rosen, Betty. *And None of It Was Nonsense: The Power of Storytelling in School.* Portsmouth, NH: Heinemann, 1988.

Ross, Eulaie, ed. "To Tell a Story." In *The Lost Half-Hour: A Collection of Stories.* New York: Harcourt, 1963.

Ross, Ramon R. *Storyteller.* Columbus, OH: Charles E. Merrill, 1972.

Rubright, Lynn. *Beyond the Beanstalk: Interdisciplinary Learning Through Storytelling.* Portsmouth, NH: Heinemann, 1996.

Sawyer, Ruth. *The Way of the Storyteller.* New York: Viking Press, 1942.

Sayers, Frances Clarke. *Summoned by Books.* New York: Viking Press, 1965.

Shedlock, Marie. *The Art of the Storyteller.* 3rd ed., rev. New York: Dover, 1951.

Shimmel, Nancy. *Just Enough to Make a Story: A Sourcebook for Storytelling.* Berkeley: Sister's Choice Press, 1982.

Sierra, Judy. *Storytellers' Research Guide: Folktales, Myths and Legends.* Eugene, OR: Folkprint, 1996.

Smith, Charles A. *From Wonder to Wisdom: Using Stories to Help Children Grow.* New York: New American Library, 1989.

Smith, Lillian. "The Art of the Fairy Tale." In *The Unreluctant Years: A Critical Approach to Children's Literature.* Chicago: American Library Association, 1953.

Sobol, Joseph. *The Storyteller's Journey: An American Revival.* Urbana: University of Illinois Press, 1999.

Spilios, Jane Baxter. *Storytelling: Physical, Verbal and Vocal Techniques.* Los Angeles: Los Angeles City College, 1960.

Stone, Kay. *Burning Brightly: New Light on Old Tales Told Today.* Peterborough, Ontario: Broadview, 1998.

Stone, Richard. *The Healing Art of Storytelling: A Sacred Journey of Personal Discovery.* New York: Hyperion, 1996.

Stotter, Ruth. *About Story: Writings on Stories and Storytelling, 1980–1994.* Stinson Beach, CA: Stotter Press, 1994.

Tanna, Laura. *Jamaican Folk Tales and Oral Histories.* Kingston, Jamaica: Institute of Jamaica Publications Limited, 1984.

Tedlock, Dennis. *The Spoken Word and the Work of Interpretation.* Philadelphia: University of Pennsylvania Press, 1983.

Tooze, Ruth. *Storytelling.* Englewood Cliffs, NJ: Prentice-Hall, 1959.

Torrence, Jackie. *Jack Tales: The Magic of Creating Stories and the Art of Telling Them.* New York: Avon, 1998.

Wolkstein, Diane. *The Magic Orange Tree and Other Haitian Folktales.* New York: Schocken Books, 1980.

Zipes, Jack. *Creative Storytelling: Building Community, Changing Lives.* New York: Routledge, 1995.

Ziskind, Sylvia. *Telling Stories to Children.* New York: Wilson, 1976.

* * * * * * * *

In *A Child's Christmas in Wales,* Dylan Thomas wrote about receiving a book that told him: "everything about the wasp, except why." The books below remind us, from a variety of perspectives, *why* stories, *why* listen, *why* tell...

Barreca, Regina. *They Used to Call Me Snow White...But I Drifted: Women's Strategic Use of Humor.* New York: Penguin Books, 1991.

Benjamin, Walter. "Reflections on the Storyteller." In *Illuminations: Essays and Reflections.* New York: Schocken Books, 1985.

Bettelheim, Bruno. *The Uses of Enchantment: The Meaning and*

Importance of Fairy Tales. New York: Knopf, 1976.

Campbell, Joseph. *The Hero with a Thousand Faces.* 2nd ed. Princeton, NJ: Princeton University Press, 1968.

Coles, Robert. *The Call of Stories: Teaching and the Moral Imagination.* Boston: Houghton Mifflin, 1989.

Estes, Clarissa Pinkola. *The Faithful Gardener: A Wise Tale about That Which Can Never Die.* San Francisco: Harper, 1995.

————. *Women Who Run with the Wolves: Myths and Stories of the Wild Woman Archetype.* New York, Balantine Books, 1992.

Fromm, Erich. *The Forgotten Language: An Introduction to the Understanding of Dreams, Fairy Tales and Myths.* New York: Holt, Rinehart and Winston, 1951.

Hyde, Lewis. *The Gift.* New York: Vintage Press, 1983.

Kane, Sean. *Wisdom of the Mythtellers.* Peterborough, Ontario: Broadview Press, 1994.

Luthi, Max. *Once Upon A Time: On the Nature of Fairy Tales.* Bloomington: Indiana University Press, 1970.

May, Rollo. *The Cry for Myth.* New York: W.W. Norton, 1991.

Myerhoff, Barbara. *Number Our Days.* New York: Simon & Schuster, 1978.

Ong, Walter J. *Orality and Literacy.* London: Routledge, 1982.

Schank, Roger C. *Tell Me a Story: A New Look at Real and Artificial Memory.* New York: Maxwell Macmillan, 1990.

Schwartz, Howard. *Reimaging the Bible: the Storytelling of the Rabbis.* New York: Oxford University Press, 1998.

Snyder, Gary. *The Practice of the Wild.* San Francisco: North Point Press, 1990.

Stone, Elizabeth. *Black Sheep and Kissing Cousins: How Our Family Stories Shape Us.* New York: Times Books, 1988.

Tatare, Maria M. *The Hard Facts of the Grimm's Fairy Tales.* Princeton, NJ: Princeton University Press, 1987.

Thompson, William Irwin. "Rapunzel: Cosmology Lost." In *Imaginary Landscape: Making Worlds of Myth and Science.* New York: St. Martin's Press, 1989.

Vansina, Jan. *Oral Tradition As History*. Madison: University of Wisconsin Press, 1985.

Von Franz, Marie-Louise. *The Feminine in Fairytales*. Irving, TX: Spring Publications, 1972.

————. *An Introduction to the Interpretation of Fairy Tales*. Irving, TX: Spring Publications, 1973.

————. *Shadow and Evil in Fairytales*. Irving, TX: Spring Publications, 1980.

Warner, Marina. *From the Beast to the Blonde: On Fairy Tales and their Tellers*. New York: Farrar Straus and Giroux, 1994.

Yolen, Jane. *Touch Magic: Fantasy, Faerie and Folklore in the Literature of Childhood*. New York: Philomel, 1981; expanded ed. Little Rock: August House, 2000.

Zeitlin, Steven J. *A Celebration of Family Folklore*. New York: Pantheon, 1982; Cambridge: Yellow Moon Press, 1992.